Engage and Empower

Engage and Empower

Expanding the Curriculum for Justice and Activism

Edited by
Mary Amanda Stewart
Christina Salazar
Victor Antonio Lozada
Christina Thomas

ROWMAN & LITTLEFIELD
Lanham • Boulder • New York • London

Published by Rowman & Littlefield
An imprint of The Rowman & Littlefield Publishing Group, Inc.
4501 Forbes Boulevard, Suite 200, Lanham, Maryland 20706
www.rowman.com

86-90 Paul Street, London EC2A 4NE, United Kingdom

Copyright © 2022 by Mary Amanda Stewart, Christina Salazar, Victor Antonio Lozada, and Christina Thomas

All rights reserved. No part of this book may be reproduced in any form or by any electronic or mechanical means, including information storage and retrieval systems, without written permission from the publisher, except by a reviewer who may quote passages in a review.

British Library Cataloguing in Publication Information Available

Library of Congress Cataloging-in-Publication Data

Names: Stewart, Mary Amanda, 1979– editor.
Title: Engage and empower : expanding the curriculum for justice and activism / edited by Mary Amanda Stewart, Christina Salazar, Victor Antonio Lozada, Christina Thomas.
Description: Lanham, Maryland : Rowman & Littlefield, 2022. | Includes bibliographical references. | Summary: "This edited book provides ready-to-use, engaging curriculum units for an integrated approach to teaching English language arts and U.S. history in grades 4–12"—Provided by publisher.
Identifiers: LCCN 2021036911 (print) | LCCN 2021036912 (ebook) | ISBN 9781475863062 (paperback) | ISBN 9781475863055 (cloth) | ISBN 9781475863079 (epub)
Subjects: LCSH: Social justice and education—United States. | Language arts (Elementary)—United States. | Language arts—Correlation with content subjects—United States.
Classification: LCC LC192.2 .E64 2022 (print) | LCC LC192.2 (ebook) | DDC 370.11/5—dc23
LC record available at https://lccn.loc.gov/2021036911
LC ebook record available at https://lccn.loc.gov/2021036912

To every student who has been ignored, devalued, and silenced.
You matter.
We value you.
May every teacher hear your beautiful voice.

Contents

Foreword ix
Tiffany A. Flowers

Introduction: Teachers Unbought and Unbossed xi
Mary Amanda Stewart

PART I: EFFECTS AND TRANSACTIONS OF EXPANSION, COLONIALISM, AND MIGRATION **1**

1 Colonialism and Native American Resiliency 3
   Patricia Flint and Mariannella Núñez

2 Modern-Day Colonialism: Washington D.C., Puerto Rico, and Other U.S. Territories 25
   Marlene Walker

3 Immigration: The Fabric of Our Nation 39
   Yismelle Duran

PART II: THE INFLUENCES OF LATIN AMERICA ON U.S. CULTURE AND SOCIETY **57**

4 Latinx Influencers: Past and Present Contributions to America's Greatness 59
   Margarita Ramos-Rivera

5 Latinas as Change Agents: Feminist Activism in the United States 71
   Juan Borda

PART III: AMERICA'S ORIGINAL SIN: UNDERSTANDING AND RESPONDING TO RACISM   87

6   Antiracism: Understanding Our History to Co-create a Better Future   89
Christina Thomas and Victor Antonio Lozada

7   Redlining: A Mechanism of Systemic Racism   103
Christina Salazar

8   Cultural (Mis)representations in the Media: Challenging Hegemonic Ideas   121
Phyliciá Anderson

PART IV: EXPLORING THE DIVERSE LIVED EXPERIENCES OF MODERN-DAY ADOLESCENTS   133

9   The Death of Childhood: Mass Shootings in the United States   135
Christina Thomas

10   Rap Music: Leveraging Hip-Hop Culture to Empower   147
Victor Antonio Lozada

11   Consent Isn't Complicated: The Implications of the #MeToo Movement   165
Christina Thomas

12   See Us: LGBTQ+ Issues for Representation, Empathy, and Justice   179
Christina Salazar

Afterword   197
Isabel Morales

About the Editors   199

About the Contributors   201

Foreword

When I was invited to write the foreword for this book, I was excited to undertake such an enormous responsibility. I was hopeful after reading several sections of this text. I knew that the authors of this work have compiled a strong collection to show what integrated content instruction looks like across grade levels with adaptable and understandable content. In my experience within the field, one of the main reasons teachers have difficulty understanding these concepts has to do with lack of readily available standards-based resource materials they can use.

In the past thirty years, there have been numerous changes to landscape of the field of education. Past theories, research, and teaching in the field of education go far beyond the initial ideas of inclusion within the curriculum, social justice frameworks, and racial representation. Current theories focus on using a variety of texts, practical strategies for studying diverse histories, and making critical conversations the norm. Many of these approaches previously include diversity work in isolation and were deemed as important. However, the previous theories, research, and practice often fell short as merely literature extensions in ELA classrooms, specialized curricula in social studies classrooms, and various interpretations of classroom inquiry. While we continue to redefine curriculum, national standards, and teaching methods within the field, we must expand our existing understanding of these concepts as well. Additionally, we must recognize quality practice related to the new theories and research in the field. As more scholars continue to produce texts which connect theory, research, and practice, we will no doubt see attempts to come to a consensus on the issues of teaching justice in English Language Arts and classrooms in practice. *Engage and Empower: Expanding the Curriculum for Justice and Activism* demonstrates a strong direction of where our work as activists and advocates can lead us regarding a need to expand the optics of the current theories, research, and practices in the field.

With this text, educators and literacy professionals now have a roadmap to follow when preparing justice-oriented lessons for children in grades 4–12. The authors of this text have done an amazing job of making abstract concepts related to social justice into practical, inquiry-based instruction. This includes but is not limited to critical literacy, implementation of diverse texts, and antiracist concepts. The notable highlights within the work include a focus on multimodal texts, hip-hop literacies, and the connection to national common core standards. I am confident this text can be used and or adapted with upper elementary, middle, and secondary students. Twenty-first-century teachers deal with issues and questions students have about gun violence, redlining in communities of color, and discussions pertaining to race in the classroom. We are long past the time when these conversations can be curtailed or avoided. Additionally, there is no room for teachers to do simple lessons about these concepts in isolation of the "regular curriculum." Teachers are in a space now where students' lived experiences are being brought to the forefront of the classroom each day. There is not a day that goes by that literacy teachers do not encounter tough questions from students. The existing curriculum is filled with difficult topics from historical movements for the establishment of rights, to contemporary issues of justice and accountability. Therefore, it is no longer acceptable to push a curriculum focus where diversity content is pulled out of a box and used in isolation. However, it is our duty as educators to begin creating real-life curricula that speak to the children; we teach within a twenty-first-century classroom. I believe *Engage and Empower* gives teachers both the tools and the empowerment to adapt this work in grades 4–12.

Tiffany A. Flowers, PhD
Georgia State University Perimeter College

Introduction
Teachers Unbought and Unbossed
Mary Amanda Stewart

Shirley Chisholm is likely someone you never learned about in your school's curriculum, nor is she regularly included in what today's adolescents are learning. Nevertheless, her campaign slogan for her 1972 presidential campaign "Unbought and Unbossed" set the stage for this book.

I admit that I did not know who Shirley Chisholm was until I inherited my grandmother's signed copy of *Unbought and Unbossed* a year ago (Figure i.1). Chisholm's words written to my grandmother, Mary Waldrop, speak to me today: "Aim high!" Chisholm's trailblazing life as the first Black woman elected to the U.S. Congress has inspired me, as I've learned more about her through FX's mini-series *Mrs. America*, her autobiography (Chisholm, 1970), as well as children's literature I'm now discovering. I understand why Phyliciá Anderson, the teacher-researcher who authored chapter 8, told us in class that Shirley Chisholm was her hero. I now understand why Chambers and Baker (2020) claim in their children's book that "Shirley Chisholm is a verb," a person of action.

In Chisholm's autobiography (1970), she asserts that our nation's young people are our hope for the future. She explains that few adults can escape socialization so deeply entwined into their thoughts, prohibiting them/us from identifying the arbitrary hierarchies based on race, class, gender, nationality, sexual orientation, and so many other factors that compound, forming intersectional forms of oppression for many people. Although we might have a waning hope that most adults will get it, there is tremendous hope for young people, youth who inspired Representative Chisholm in the 1970s and inspire us in the 2020s. The words she used to describe young people decades ago, still ring true today:

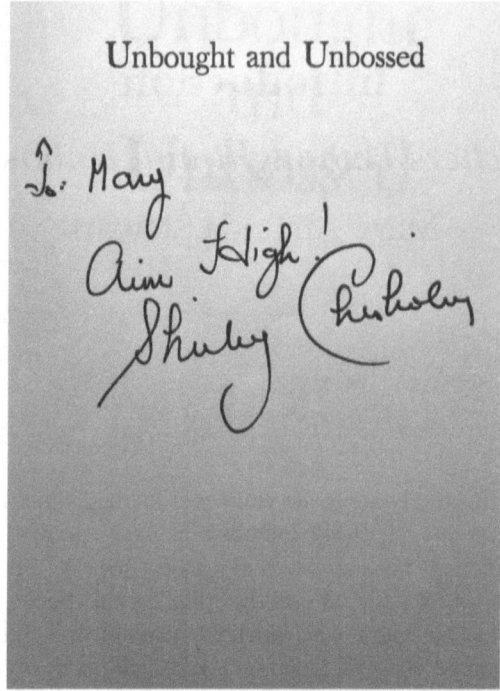

Figure I.1 Signed Copy of *Unbought and Unbossed*.

Most young people are not yet revolutionary, but politicians and police and other persons in power almost seem to be conspiring to turn them into revolutionaries. Like me, I think, most of them are no more revolutionary than the founders of this country. Their goals are the same—to insure individual liberty and equality of opportunity and forever to thwart the tyrannous tendencies of government, which inevitably arise from the arrogance and isolation of men who are securely in power. All they want, if it were not too unfashionable for them to say so, is for the American dream to come true, at least in its less materialistic aspect. . . . 'Liberty and justice for all' were beautiful words, but the ugly fact was that liberty and justice were only for white males. How incredible that nearly 200 years since then, and we have still to fight the same old enemies! (p. 171–172)

The young people in the United States today repeat or at least hear those same words, "with liberty and justice for all," every day in their schools. Educators need to help them understand the meaning of this statement through a historical context to recognize the unequal nuances of what it means in our modern society. Our English language arts and social studies classrooms are prime places to start.

Yet, our educational system is a product of our society, dealing with the same systems of oppression and power (Love, 2019). There are those that want to privatize it—to buy it (Ravitch, 2011). This occurs as testing companies control our curriculum, buying what is taught in the classroom. Further, teachers and administrators often feel bossed, being told what to teach as determined by what others deem important, usually tied back to those testing companies who are buying our educational system (Gilbert, 2014).

However, the teacher-researchers who authored the curriculum units in this book are truly unbought and unbossed. Like Shirley Chisholm, they believe that young people should know more about U.S. history than what is explicitly included in the standards or state-adopted curriculum. They believe that their students, who primarily come from minoritized communities, should see themselves in the curriculum. These teacher-researchers, who almost all also come from the same minoritized communities, are not afraid of teaching the difficult parts in our distant or even recent histories, knowing that young people need spaces in schools, *deserve* spaces, to make sense of systemic racism, modern-day gun violence, and so much more than they have inherited.

THE PURPOSE OF THE BOOK

Therefore, in this book, teacher-researchers provide ready-to-use, engaging curriculum units for an integrated approach to teaching English language arts and U.S. history in grades 4–12. Their purpose is to promote social justice and activism through the educational system while building critical literacies students need in the twenty-first century. By implementing the curriculum units in this book, teachers and students can challenge inequities and promote activism. Each unit (chapter) contains a theme that is relevant to historical and modern events in the United States, particularly timely social problems.

A central goal of this project is to represent and empower marginalized students. The U.S. history that is deemed by those in power to be worthy of study or essential knowledge is limited and only represents one view of history, privileging the experiences of White people. In this book, the authors intentionally center the experiences of Black, Indigenous, People of Color (BIPOC) and other marginalized communities, teaching literacy through an emancipatory lens. Freire and Macedo (1987) describe emancipatory literacy as an awareness of the histories, experiences, and cultures of historically oppressed individuals accompanied by the agency to act. In addition to expanding the curriculum to include more people, educating students about issues of injustice in the United States will enable them to become agents of change. If students are able to understand the foundations and current iterations of present-day inequities, they will be better positioned to question and challenge future injustices. After all, the history of oppression is the foundation for modern oppression including racism, patriarchy and any form of discrimination or thought. and any form of discrimination or thought. The units presented in this book serve to illuminate the work of the oppressed in freeing themselves, thereby laying the foundation for our students to do the same emancipatory work (Freire, 1998).

Finally, the teacher-researchers authoring these chapters hope that students who are more privileged will benefit from exposure to these issues. Unquestioning, yet everyday people carry out oppression (Applebaum, 2008). Many Americans who are participating in injustices are not extremists nor obvious racists. Most are average citizens who are unquestioning. They are good people who have accepted modern, sometimes invisible, systems of oppression as natural and normal. By creating space for alternative perspectives, the authors aim to reduce the friction that occurs when encountering diverse, often conflicting, perspectives based on one's different lived experiences in the world. By educating students about the privileges they have not examined, teachers can empower allies.

Yet this is difficult to accomplish for most teachers. Thus, the authors have outlined ready-to-use units that connect to the Common Core State Standards (CCSS) for both English language arts and U.S. history. They explain how teachers (novice and veteran) can use these units and modify the curriculum and instructional approaches for their particular students.

HOW TO USE THE BOOK

The book contains twelve chapters, each focusing on a different curriculum unit that could last up to six weeks, yet can also be useful for a shorter amount of time. The themes focus on current issues in social justice and blind spots in the modern history curriculum. Each of the twelve chapters is authored by one or more teacher-researchers with practicality in mind. Through their experience in the classroom, they know what you might be up against as you try to expand the curriculum. Pushback from students, other teachers, administrators, and parents is real and should be expected by anyone wanting to create positive change. Consequently, they begin each chapter by providing a compelling, research-supported, rationale for their theme and teaching ideas. These rationales serve to support teachers and administrators who may receive questions about changes to curriculum and the inclusion of sensitive topics.

In order to facilitate the implementation of these curriculum units, each chapter details lesson plans that teachers can immediately apply in their classrooms. The lessons include adaptations for application across grade levels and accommodations for special populations. Then, to strengthen the justification of these lessons, they align with the CCSS. Each chapter follows the same format, containing the following primary features.

Usability and Practicality

The teacher-researchers designed each unit to provide ready-to-use lessons and teaching ideas to engage their students by expanding the curriculum. Teachers will be able to easily select a unit to use with their students then quickly navigate to resources that will facilitate the implementation. There are at least two detailed lesson plans for each unit, and teachers can use the text set and other teaching ideas to create their own lessons for their unique group of students.

Multimodal Text Set

Each unit contains a multimodal text set which is a collection of print, audio, image, and video resources appropriate for adolescents to deeply engage with the theme. These have been carefully curated by practicing teachers and a school librarian. They include many award-winning children's, adolescent, and young adult literature as well as online reading from reputable sources such as Newsela and supporting videos. This multimodal text set provides the curriculum that the teacher draws from in order to create a multi-week unit of instruction.

Connection to CCSS

Each unit includes CCSS that support the teaching ideas from the English language arts and social studies (e.g., U.S. history and geography) as well as other disciplines. This provides teachers and curriculum specialists with rationales for using this innovative curricular approach and assists them in writing and submitting their lesson plans.

Multilingual Resources

Understanding the great linguistic diversity in the United States, the multilingual teacher-contributors to this book have purposefully included texts and other resources that are available in many languages other than English. These multilingual resources make these units applicable to the bilingual, dual language, English as a second language, and world language classroom in addition to the English-medium classroom with multilingual students such as emergent bilinguals or heritage language speakers. In fact, many of the teacher-contributors are practicing in bilingual and world language classrooms where they deliver instruction in Spanish and French in addition to English. All of them teach in a context with many emergent bilinguals from different language backgrounds as well. The English-medium teacher in a linguistically diverse classroom can leverage the multilingual resources to help students develop their knowledge and literacy in their home language in addition to English.

Assessment and Evaluation Tools

Understanding that providing student feedback and grades is an essential component for all educators, authors provide rubrics and other assessment criteria for the main assignments in each unit.

BOOK ORGANIZATION

Each of these teacher-researchers chose a topic close to their heart, often from their own lived experiences. Some of these units are about ideas or people they wish they would have learned about in school. Other units are parts of our history the authors want their own students (and children) to more deeply understand. The twelve chapters are divided into four parts that center on a common idea. Therefore, teachers could potentially spend an entire semester, deeply exploring a larger idea through multiple units.

Part I explores the effects and transactions of expansion, colonialism, and migration. It begins with Patricia Flint and Mariannella Núñez's chapter on the beginning of colonialism in this land and the resiliency of First Nations Peoples. Connected to this topic through her daughter-in-law and grandchildren, "Tricia," along with former bilingual/ESL teacher "Marie," invites teachers to teach their students about past events that influence modern phenomena such as the Standing Rock protests and the #NotYourMascot campaign. Then, in chapter 2, readers will meet a bilingual teacher with years of practice, Marlene Walker, as she shares a very personal unit from her lived experiences of being a proud Puerto Rican living in the United States. She also includes connections to other territories, knowing that the statehood of Washington, D.C. is currently in the news and will continue to be a relevant political topic. Finally, part I concludes with another teacher-researcher with personal experience regarding her theme. Señora or Madame Duran, as her Spanish and French high school students might call her, recently moved to the United States from the Dominican Republic, experiencing firsthand the immigration she discusses while also drawing from her students' stories of family migration.

Part II celebrates the cultural heritage of most of the authors in this book who identify as Latina, Latino, or Latinx as well as the majority of the students they teach. In chapter 4, Margarita Ramos-Rivera, also from Puerto Rico and who teaches bilingual Latinx 4th graders, created a unit meant to give her students pride in themselves. She guides them to learn about people from their diverse Latinx communities who have made great contributions to this country. Then, in chapter 5, veteran bilingual teacher Juan Borda shares a unit on historical and modern Latina activists in the United States who are effecting change in various ways.

Part III is perhaps the heartbeat of this book which the authors and I began writing in an adolescent literacy course where we all read *Stamped from the Beginning: Racism, Antiracism, and You* (Kendi & Reynolds, 2020), followed by *Just Mercy* (Stevenson, 2015). This shared experience changed us all in some way and lit the fire for us to accept a call to action to "teach the change we wish to see." Consequently, chapter 6 was born out of a challenge in class. Working in groups, we gave ourselves one hour to create as much of a curriculum unit as possible based on our own transformative reading about racism. Collaboratively sharing our knowledge of resources, standards, and ideas, we put together a good draft that two of the book editors, Christina Thomas and Victor Antonio Lozada polished. (I think we might all agree that if you only teach one unit of this book, teach this one. But we hope you'll teach them all!) Then, our resident school librarian and former high school teacher, Christina Salazar, helps us further investigate racism through the practice of redlining in chapter 7. Although students might have heard this term in the news, they might not really understand how it works to invisibly perpetuate racism. In chapter 8, Phyliciá Anderson connects to every student, teacher, or person who has felt misrepresented by media portrayals of people who look like them. Through her expertise in journalism and critical literacy, she guides teachers to work with their students to interrogate the messages they receive from media sources and how those can work to sustain racist and other discriminatory ideologies.

In part IV, the goal is to "keep it real" and connect to young people's worlds today. In chapter 9, Christina Thomas, one of our youngest teacher-researchers, delves into a difficult yet needed topic, gun violence and mass shootings in the United States. This is a defining issue of her generation as well as the current generation of adolescent students. Her highly engaging unit provides a way for teachers to bring this difficult topic into the classroom for students to express their fears, frustrations, and opinions. Knowing that many difficult issues are present in rap music, Victor Lozada, a bilingual music educator, authors chapter 10 to illustrate the power that rap music has specifically, and hip-hop culture generally, to empower young people, provide them a space to share their voice, make sense of their world, and even engage in activism. Then, in chapter 11, Christina Thomas presents another difficult, yet needed topic in the age of #MeToo. Although geared for older learners, she even shows how teachers might approach this relevant issue with younger students through purposeful text selections and discussion approaches. Finally, Christina Salazar gives voice to LGBTQ+ students in chapter 12, illustrating that teachers can teach what some might deem sensitive topics such as sexuality and gender identity while connecting to the standards. From historic discrimination of LGBTQ+ people in the United States to modern-day triumphs such as the Marriage Equality Act, this unit will provide some students a needed "I see you" while affording others a glimpse into someone's life. This might prompt greater understanding and empathy for one another, a truly needed change in our society.

CALL TO ACTION

The units in this book represent authors' unique contributions to the movements for equality and justice currently happening in the United States, often led by young people. This is their declaration that they are teachers who are unbought and unbossed, compelled to teach what they hold important, even necessary. I invite you, dear readers, to join them, channeling your inner Shirley Chisholm, charting a new course in your school.

Is it hard? Yes. Will there be a pushback? Probably. Will you feel alone? Likely. This is an uphill battle that you might not be willing to do for yourself, but we ask you to do it for your students so the next generation is not only more kind and compassionate but more just and driven to action.

Join us in being teachers unbought and unbossed!

REFERENCES

Applebaum, B. (2008). White privilege/White complicity: Connecting "benefiting from" to "contributing to." In R. D. Glass (Ed.) *Philosophy of Education yearbook*. (pp. 292–300) Philosophy of Education. https://educationjournal.web.illinois.edu/archive/index.php/pes/article/view/1380.pdf.

Chambers, V., & Baker, R. (2020). *Shirley Chisholm is a verb!* Dial Books for Young Readers.

Chisholm, S. (1970). *Unbought and unbossed.* Houghton Mifflin.

Freire, P. (1998). *Teachers as cultural workers: Letters to those who dare teach.* Westview Press.

Freire, P., & Macedo, D. P. (1987). *Literacy: Reading the word and the world.* Bergin & Garvey Publishers.

Gilbert, C. (2014). A call for subterfuge: Shielding the ELA classroom from the restrictive sway of the Common Core. *English Journal, 104*(2), 27–33.

Kendi, I. X., & Reynolds, J. (2020). *Stamped: Racism, antiracism, and you* (first ed.). Little, Brown and Company.

Love, B. L. (2019). *We want to do more than survive: Abolitionist teaching and the pursuit of educational freedom.* Beacon Press.

Ravitch, D. (2011). *The death and life of the great American school system: How testing and choice are undermining education* (rev. and expanded ed.). Basic Books.

Stevenson, B. (2015). *Just mercy: A story of justice and redemption.* Spiegel & Grau.

Part I

EFFECTS AND TRANSACTIONS OF EXPANSION, COLONIALISM, AND MIGRATION

Figure P1.1 Mors Feminorum. *Briana Carter.*

Their land was stolen. But, in July 2020, the Supreme Court began doing what Tuck and Yang (2012) said that we must do: give it back. While it was only the tiniest portion of the land that was stolen, almost half of the land in eastern Oklahoma now belongs to five tribes. Now they get to decide what is (and is not) done on their land. How people move into, around, and from the United States through immigration and migration gives historical context to the land—and power—stealing in our country. Examining these past (and present) wrongdoings is central to understanding how current political and environmental forces affect the migration patterns of all humans.

The following section brings to light the subjugated histories of colonized people including Native Americans, citizens of the United States such as the residents of Washington, D.C., and Puerto Rico, and the history of how the many people of the world came to the United States for freedom only to be met as second-class citizens. We hope that your students will come to appreciate the many histories of the forgotten people of the land that is now called the United States.

Tuck, E., & Yang, K. W. (2012). Decolonization is not a metaphor. *Decolonization: Indigeneity, Education, and Society, 1*(1), 1–40.

Chapter 1

Colonialism and Native American Resiliency

Patricia Flint and Mariannella Núñez

Figure 1.1 The Keep. *Florence Boachie.*

THEME AND RATIONALE

The history of the United States is often limited to social studies or history courses where the focus is on recalling important figures, dates, and events, which were typically deemed important by groups of White men. This unit extends beyond the historical parameters intended for those courses and focuses on the critical development of students through reading and writing. It is appropriate to begin the collection of justice-focused teaching units with the topic of colonialism, as it is foundational to understanding the inequities and injustices before us today.

Colonialism is not strictly a modern occurrence. History is full of examples of one society growing its empire by occupying adjacent or distant territories and settling its people in the new territory. According to Webster's Encyclopedic Unabridged Dictionary of the English Language (1989), "Colonialism is the policy of a country seeking to extend or retain its authority over other people or territories" (n.p.). In the process of colonization, colonizers may force their religion, economics, and other cultural practices onto the Indigenous peoples.

Interestingly, the earliest use of the words *colony* and *colonization* began in agriculture and not in military domination (Encyclopedia of American Studies, 2018). When a colony was planted, it was then referred to as a plantation. Before the arrival of the Europeans to North America, America was thought to be wild and inhabited by savages who were not properly using their resources. The Europeans felt it was their divine duty to control this land, use it properly, and convert the savages to the European way of life. Colonization left a legacy of slavery and Indian removal.

It is also important to recognize that civilization did not begin with colonialism. We should honor the Indigenous peoples who thrived on the land now called the United States. In understanding the unfiltered past of our country, students can begin to understand how these events impact our thinking, actions, and attitudes. Educators have traditionally taught colonialism by addressing the causes, the effects, and the places of colonialism, as well as the Anglo men involved. Students are infrequently afforded the opportunity, time, or resources to learn from the perspectives of the Indigenous peoples who were, and continue to be, negatively affected, yet still manage to thrive in various ways, illustrating their resiliency.

UNIT GOALS

This unit will allow educators to use a critical literacy stance to address the theme of colonialism through the perspectives of the Indigenous people. Included in this unit are multimodal text options, as well as ideas on how to accommodate emergent bilinguals, students with special needs, and students of varying grade levels. The goal of this chapter is not only to create a unit that makes learning equitable for all students but also to offer a unique way of teaching colonialism by privileging the perspectives of people who are often marginalized and even silenced through multiple instructional texts. As teachers, we are called to action by the words of Eagle Shield et al. (2020): "Social movements are not exceptional and not isolated events; they are persistent resistance by ordinary actors with generations of teachers and students before and after them" (p. xiii).

MULTIMODAL TEXT SET

The resources presented here are intended to support classroom exploration of topics about colonialism and Native American resiliency. Several of these texts are included in the sample lessons while additional resources are provided for individual student projects and flexibility. There are more applications of these texts than those presented in the sample lessons. For example, any of these resources can be used to spark classroom discussion, introduce or close a lesson, or provide additional resources for students who are working ahead of schedule or who want to explore the issues further. Other possibilities include providing selection opportunities of particular texts to different students, differentiating based on strengths and interests, and asking students to present their learning to the class or a group. Teachers can include a choice board of presentation options to reflect students' strengths and comfort. For example, some students may be comfortable giving a slide presentation while others would rather create a website, video, or pamphlet to share their findings. As classroom experts, teachers should not feel limited to the suggested uses in this chapter.

Illustrated Children's Books

- Jameson, C., & Flett, J. (2006). *Zoe and the fawn*. Theytus Books.
- Maillard, K. N., & Martinez-Neal, J. (2019). *Fry bread: A Native American family story*. Roaring Brook Press.
- Messinger, C., Katz, S., & Fadden, D. K. (2007). *When the shadbush blooms*. Tricycle Press.
- Minnema, C., & Flett, J. (2019). *Johnny's pheasant*. University of Minnesota Press.
- Robertson, D. A., & Flett, J. (2016). *When we were alone*. HighWater Press.
- Smith, C. L., Hu, Y. H., & Van Wright, C. (2000). *Jingle dancer*. William Morrow.
- Tahe, R. A., Flood, N. B., & Nelson, J. (2018). *First laugh: Welcome baby*. Charlesbridge Publishing.

- Tudor, A., Tudor, K., & Eaglespeaker, J. (2018). *Young water protectors: A story about standing rock.* CreateSpace Independent Publishing Platform.
- Vermette, K., & Flett, J. (2019). *The girl and the wolf.* Theytus Books.

Chapter Books

- Alexie, S. (2001). *The toughest Indian in the world.* Grove Press.
- Alexie, S. (2005). *The Lone Ranger and Tonto fistfight in heaven.* Grove Press.
- Eastman, C. (2003). *From the deep woods to civilization.* Dover Publications.
- Eastman, C. (2008). *Indian boyhood.* Dover.
- Echo-Hawk, W. (2018). *The sea of grass: A family tale from the heartland.* Fulcrum Publishing.
- Glancy, D. (1996). *Pushing the bear: A novel of the trail of tears.* Houghton Mifflin.
- Hale, J. C. (1998). *Bloodlines: Odyssey of a native daughter.* University of Arizona Press.
- LaDuke, W. (2008). *All our relations: Native struggles for land and life.* South End Press.
- Tingle, T. (2014). *House of purple cedar.* Cinco Puntos Press.
- Vizenor, G. (2010). *Shrouds of white earth.* Excelsior Editions/State University of New York Press.
- Welch, J. (1986). *Winter in the blood.* Penguin Books.
- Yahgulanaas, M. N. (2014). *Red: A Haida manga.* Douglas & McIntyre.

Poetry

- Harjo, J. (2001). *A map to the next world: Poetry and tales.* W. W. Norton Company.
- northSun, N. (2007). *Love at gunpoint.* R. L. Crow Publications.
- Rose, W. (1994). *Bone dance: New and selected poems, 1965–1993.* University of Arizona Press.

Informational Text

- Chow, K. (February 9, 2018). So what exactly is "blood quantum"? https://www.npr.org/sections/codeswitch/2018/02/09/583987261/so-what-exactly-is-blood-quantum
- Earthjustice (March 25, 2020). Standing Rock Sioux tribe prevails as federal judge strikes down DAPL permits. https://earthjustice.org/news/press/2020/standing-rock-sioux-tribe-prevails-as-federal-judge-strikes-down-dapl-permits

- Editors of Encyclopedia Britannica (July 20, 1998). Indian reorganization act. https://www.britannica.com/topic/Indian-Reorganization-Act
- Encyclopedia.com (May 18, 2018). New Mexico. https://www.encyclopedia.com/places/united-states-and-canada/us-political-geography/new-mexico
- Encylopedia.com (May 29, 2018). Internal colonialism. https://www.encyclopedia.com/social-sciences-and-law/sociology-and-social-reform/sociology-general-terms-and-concepts/internal-colonialism
- Friedman, L. (March 25, 2020). Standing Rock Sioux Tribe wins a victory in Dakota access pipeline case. https://www.nytimes.com/2020/03/25/climate/dakota-access-pipeline-sioux.html
- Gallay, A. (October 27, 2015). Settlement: Native American slavery in the Americas. *Newsela.com*.
- Hair, J. (April 27, 2016). What is "blood quantum"? | definition, facts, laws | Native American Indian. https://www.powwows.com/native-american-blood-quantum-facts-and-myths/#:~:text=Blood%20quantum%20is%20the%20measurement,used%20to%20determine%20tribal%20enrollment.
- Murphy, J. & Chavez, W. (June 22, 2020). June 22, 1839: A bloody day in Cherokee nation. https://www.cherokeephoenix.org/culture/june-22-1839-a-bloody-day-in-cherokee-nation/article_6254b899-f25e-5f73-b23a-839e3b6ce00a.html
- Nagle, R. (December 1, 2019). Opinion: Half the land in Oklahoma could be returned to Native Americans. *Newsela.com*
- National Archives (August 15, 2016). American Indian Urban Relocation. https://www.archives.gov/education/lessons/indian-relocation.html
- Newsela staff (April 20, 2017). Colonial America depended on the enslavement of Indigenous people. *Newsela.com*.
- Newsela staff (May 24, 2017). Overview of Native American and colonial relations. *Newsela.com*.
- Newsela staff (July 15, 2020). Washington's NFL team drops its name after eighty-seven years. *Newslea.com*
- Newsela staff (July 22, 2020). Justices rule swath of Oklahoma remains tribal reservation. *Newsela.com*.
- Newsela staff (November 5, 2020). Native American women shape how museums frame Indigenous culture. *Newsela.com*.
- Rose, A. (April 30, 2015). The exploitation of colonialism. https://people.smu.edu/knw2399/2015/04/30/the-exploitation-of-colonialism/
- Smithsonian Institution (2018). Treaties still matter: The Dakota access pipeline. https://americanindian.si.edu/nk360/plains-treaties/dapl
- South African History Online (February 1, 2012). A Heritage trail through the provinces of South Africa. https://www.sahistory.org.za/article/grade-5-term-4-heritage-trail-through-provinces-south-africa
- The Living New Deal (n.d.). Indian reorganization act (1934). https://livingnewdeal.org/glossary/indian-reorganization-act-1934/

- Wilma, D. (August 12, 2000). Wheeler-Howard act (Indian Reorganization Act) shifts U.S. policy toward Native American right to self-determination on June 18, 1934. https://www.historylink.org/File/2599#:~:text=On%20June%2018%2C%201934%2C%20the,self%2Ddetermination%20for%20Native%20Americans

Videos

- Native American Elder Nathan Phillips, teen Nick Sandmann give versions of encounter: YouTube
- The Word Indigenous Explained: YouTube
- Uprooted: The 1950's plan to erase Indian Country: apmreports.org
- W.O.W. Internal Colonialism: YouTube

Images

- Standing Rock: Find several publicly available images on Google when searching "Standing Rock" such as Figure 1.2 found at https://thepetroglyph.com/big-money-pulling-the-strings-at-the-standing-rock-pipeline-protest-8c1f638283dc
- Colonialism: Find several publicly available images on Google when searching "Colonialism" such as Figure 1.3 found at https://www.youtube.com/watch?v=jp3ClAYgyp8

Websites for Recommended Native American Books:

- Native American Children's Literature Recommended Reading List: first-nations.org
- Twenty #ownvoices Children's Books About Native Americans and First Nations Canadians: rebekahgienapp.com
- American Indians in Children's Literature: americanindiansinchildrensliterature.blogspot.com
- Thirty-two Native American Children's Books: coloursofus.com
- Native American Heritage Month: lapl.org
- The Open Book Blog: blog.leeandlow.com

Websites

- American Public Media: www.apmreports.org
- Britannica.com: https://www.britannica.com/place/Oklahoma-state/History

Figure 1.2 Example Standing Rock Image.

Figure 1.3 Example Colonialism Image.

- National Indigenous Women's Resource Center: Niwrc.org
- National Museum of the American Indian: https://americanindian.si.edu/nk360
- Edges of Empire: People.smu.edu

Additional Texts for Further Learning

For educators wanting further reading on colonialism, there are several options to consider. For an overview of colonialism, see *How Colonialism Works* on howstuffworks.com which provides a brief overview of colonialism and some of its effects. The National Geographic website offers a great article—*What Is Colonialism?*—with links to various other resources for learning more about this topic. *Colonialism, Explained*, from the website teenvogue.com, is an article that sheds light on the two significant waves of colonialism in history. Also, you won't want to miss out on the informative links to other relevant topics that this article offers.

For further learning about Indigenous peoples, try starting with the fact sheet *Who Are Indigenous People?* from the website United Nations Permanent Forum on Indigenous Issues, https://www.un.org/esa/socdev/unpfii/documents/5session_factsheet1.pdf. It offers some basic definitions and ideas. Videos can also be great sources of information, such as *I am Indigenous* and *Protecting the Rights and Wellbeing of Indigenous Peoples* from youtube.com. These videos share the voices and perspectives of many of the world's Indigenous peoples.

For further learning on contemporary instances of colonialism and its effects on Indigenous peoples, chapters 5–8 of *Education in Movement Spaces: Standing Rock to Chicago Freedom Square* offer the perspectives of the people directly involved in the movement at Standing Rock to block the Dakota Access Pipeline from being constructed on Native lands. These activists and scholars discuss the effects of this fight on the Native people living on these lands and how they all worked together to block the further taking of their lands and water while creating education spaces within the movement. The Defenders of the Water School was established at the movement's encampment. These education spaces at the school provided a decolonial way of educating the young in their home language and ways of living that did not involve Western standards.

A final source for further learning is the article titled "Why a Former Olympic Site Is Finally Removing this Native American Slur from Its Name" by Aishwarya Kumar. This article addresses some mature issues that Native Americans (in some instances, exclusively Native American women) have been facing for centuries. While this article is suitable for educator learning, it can be used for high school students learning as well. See www.squawalpine.com.

com/name-change for some novel and highly enlightening information about how the resort area was renamed.

SAMPLE LESSONS

Table 1.1 contains an overview of the unit with general teaching ideas that correspond to the standards. Below are some sample lessons to use during the unit.

Sample Lesson One: Introduction to Colonialism

This is an appropriate lesson to begin the unit on colonialism and Native American resiliency. Students will understand colonialism and some of its effects.

Whole Group

1. Start the unit with a whole group discussion about colonialism to determine what your students already know about the term and to activate any prior knowledge. Ask the following questions: "Have you heard this word before? If yes, where did you hear or see it?" This will help you understand your students' context for this word. If they do not know this term ask: "Look at the word colonialism. Is there a smaller word inside that you may know?" This will help them determine some meaning for the term.
2. Next, present the following definition: *Colonialism* is the theory, "We are superior to everyone else so that means that we have the right to take over their land and run it for our own benefit" (Webster's Encyclopedia of the English Language, 1989, p. 291). *Colonialism* is the theory that leads to *Colonization*. Then ask, "How do these ideas fit with what we just discussed?". Then, watch the video on "Colonialism": *https://www.youtube.com/watch?v=wjigi-ObCzE*.

Small Group

1. Continue by grouping the class into small groups or partners and pass out the Newsela article (available in Spanish and various reading levels): *Scholarly Analysis: Western Civilization's Legacy Has a Dark Side*: https://newsela.com/read/lib-convo-dark-side-of-western-civilization/id/29331/activities?collection_id=339&search_id=b7d25267-acb9-4f9c-a420-9fee16d1ae07.

Table 1.1 Unit Overview and General Teaching Ideas

Week One: While this unit is intended for 5th grade students, it can be modified for other grade levels.

- Early Colonialism
  - Settler
  - Exploitation/Enslavement
  - Surrogate
  - Internal

Common Core Standards	Some Related Texts/Resources

• CCSS.ELA-LITERACY.RI.5.1
Quote accurately from a text when explaining what the text says explicitly and when drawing inferences from the text.
• CCSS.ELA-LITERACY.RI.5.2
Determine two or more main ideas of a text and explain how they are supported by key details; summarize the text.
• CCSS.ELA-LITERACY.RI.5.3
Explain the relationships or interactions between two or more individuals, events, ideas, or concepts in a historical, scientific, or technical text based on specific information in the text.
• CCSS.ELA-LITERACY.RI.5.5
Compare and contrast the overall structure (e.g., chronology, comparison, cause/effect, problem/solution) of events, ideas, concepts, or information in two or more texts.
• CCSS.ELA-LITERACY.RI.5.6
Analyze multiple accounts of the same event or topic, noting important similarities and differences in the point of view they represent.
• CCSS.ELA-LITERAvCY.RI.5.7
Draw on information from multiple print or digital sources, demonstrating the ability to quickly locate an answer to a question or to solve a problem efficiently.
	• Settler
	   o Overview of Native American and colonial relations: https://newsela.com/read/lib-overview-native-american-colonization/id/30830/?collection_id=339&search_id=8bc20a85-9a13-4f13-bf6a-7d9245c74ee6
	• Exploitation
	   o Colonial America Depended on the Enslavement of Indigenous People: https://newsela.com/read/smi-colonial-america-native-american-slaves/id/29431/?collection_id=339&search_id=ed5a03a0-b4f4-49b2-b4d3-55e7ba7635e5
	   o The Exploitation of Colonialism: https://people.smu.edu/knw2399/2015/04/30/the-exploitation-of-colonialism/
	   o Settlement: Native American Slavery in the Americas: https://newsela.com/read/gl-history-Indian-Slavery-in-the-Americas/id/22303/?collection_id=339&search_id=f151a6ba-509f-4b75-b665-82ba3e4c78e9
	   o Internal Colonialism: https://www.encyclopedia.com/social-sciences-and-law/sociology-and-social-reform/sociology-general-terms-and-concepts/internal-colonialism

Colonialism and Native American Resiliency

- CCSS.ELA-LITERACY.RI.5.8
Explain how an author uses reasons and evidence to support particular points in a text, identifying which reasons and evidence support which point(s).
- CCSS.ELA-LITERACY.RI.5.9
Integrate information from several texts on the same topic to write or speak about the subject knowledgeably.

Week Two
- Tribal Nation & U.S. Government Dynamics
  - Quantum
  - Indian Reorganization Act of 1934
  - The Reorganization Act
  - The Indian Relocation Act of 1956
  - Indigenous People's Month

Common Core Standards	Some Related Texts/Resources
• CCSS.ELA-LITERACY.RI.5.1 Quote accurately from a text when explaining what the text says explicitly and when drawing inferences from the text. • CCSS.ELA-LITERACY.RI.5.2 Determine two or more main ideas of a text and explain how they are supported by key details; summarize the text. • CCSS.ELA-LITERACY.RI.5.3 Explain the relationships or interactions between two or more individuals, events, ideas, or concepts in a historical, scientific, or technical text based on specific information in the text. • CCSS.ELA-LITERACY.RI.5.5 Compare and contrast the overall structure (e.g., chronology, comparison, cause/effect, problem/solution) of events, ideas, concepts, or information in two or more texts. • CCSS.ELA-LITERACY.RI.5.6 Analyze multiple accounts of the same event or topic, noting important similarities and differences in the point of view they represent.	• So What Exactly Is "Blood Quantum"? https://www.npr.org/sections/codeswitch/2018/02/09/583987261/so-what-exactly-is-blood-quantum • What is "Blood Quantum"? | Definition, Facts, Laws | Native American Indian: https://www.powwows.com/native-american-blood-quantum-facts-and-myths/ • June 22, 1839: A bloody day in Cherokee Nation: https://www.cherokeephoenix.org/Article/index/9300 • Indian Reorganization Act: https://www.britannica.com/topic/Indian-Reorganization-Act • Indian Reorganization Act (1934): https://livingnewdeal.org/glossary/indian-reorganization-act-1934/ • Wheeler-Howard Act (Indian Reorganization Act) shifts U.S. policy toward Native American right to self-determination on June 18, 1934: https://www.historylink.org/File/2599 • American Indian Urban Relocation: https://www.archives.gov/education/lessons/indian-relocation.html

(Continued)

Table 1.1 Unit Overview and General Teaching Ideas (*Continued*)

• CCSS.ELA-LITERACY.RI.5.7 Draw on information from multiple print or digital sources, demonstrating the ability to quickly locate an answer to a question or to solve a problem efficiently. • CCSS.ELA-LITERACY.RI.5.8 Explain how an author uses reasons and evidence to support particular points in a text, identifying which reasons and evidence support which point(s). • CCSS.ELA-LITERACY.RI.5.9 Integrate information from several texts on the same topic in order to write or speak about the subject knowledgeably.	• Uprooted: The 1950s plan to erase the Indian Country: https://www.apmreports.org/episode/2019/11/01/uprooted-the-1950s-plan-to-erase-indian-country • Native American women shape how museums frame Indigenous culture: https://newsela.com/read/indigenous-women-museum-exhibits/id/2001014203/?utm_source=aotd&utm_medium=email&utm_campaign=test-1&utm_content=news-2 • Native American elder Nathan Phillips and teen Nick Sandmann give versions of encounter: https://www.youtube.com/watch?v=0JMkzakXgIY • A Heritage trail through the provinces of South Africa: https://www.sahistory.org.za/article/grade-5-term-4-heritage-trail-through-provinces-south-africa • Washington's NFL team drops its name after eighty-seven years: https://newsela.com/read/washington-nfl-drops-name/id/2001010970/?utm_source=aotd&utm_medium=email&utm_campaign=test-1&utm_content=news-1 • Justices rule swath of Oklahoma remains tribal reservation: https://newsela.com/read/oklahoma-ruled-tribal-reservation/id/2001010978/?utm_source=aotd&utm_medium=email&utm_campaign=test-1&utm_content=news-1 • The Native history of Indigenous Peoples Day: https://www.yesmagazine.org/social-justice/2020/10/09/indigenous-peoples-day-history/ • How do we reclaim history? https://email.nationalgeographic.com/H/2/v60000017S1e15f05f9d1c036e965fd798/fa62d187-8da0-45ec-ad95-e14e26719b77/HTML • Native American seeds being reunited with their tribes: https://newsela.com/read/indigenous-tribes-reunite-seeds/id/2001013408/?utm_source=aotd&utm_medium=email&utm_campaign=test-1&utm_content=news-1

Colonialism and Native American Resiliency 15

- **Week Three**
- Land stealing
  - Standing Rock
  - Pipelines
  - Environmental
  - Mount Rushmore
  - Stone Mountain

Common Core Standards	Some Related Texts/Resources

• CCSS.ELA-LITERACY.RI.5.1
Quote accurately from a text when explaining what the text says explicitly and when drawing inferences from the text.
• CCSS.ELA-LITERACY.RI.5.2
Determine two or more main ideas of a text and explain how they are supported by key details; summarize the text.
• CCSS.ELA-LITERACY.RI.5.3
Explain the relationships or interactions between two or more individuals, events, ideas, or concepts in a historical, scientific, or technical text based on specific information in the text.
• CCSS.ELA-LITERACY.RI.5.5
Compare and contrast the overall structure (e.g., chronology, comparison, cause/effect, problem/solution) of events, ideas, concepts, or information in two or more texts.
• CCSS.ELA-LITERACY.RI.5.6
Analyze multiple accounts of the same event or topic, noting important similarities and differences in the point of view they represent.
• CCSS.ELA-LITERACY.RI.5.7
Draw on information from multiple print or digital sources, demonstrating the ability to quickly locate an answer to a question or to solve a problem efficiently.
	• Standing Rock History: https://www.standingrock.org/content/history
	• Standing Rock Sioux Tribe Prevails as Federal Judge Strikes Down DAPL Permits: https://earthjustice.org/news/press/2020/standing-rock-sioux-tribe-prevails-as-federal-judge-strikes-down-dapl-permits?gclid=EAIaIQobChMIrOPg4LSn6gIVT9bACh1IqA5IEAAYASAAEgKPBD_BwE
	• Standing Rock Sioux Tribe Wins a Victory in Dakota Access Pipeline Case: https://www.nytimes.com/2020/03/25/climate/dakota-access-pipeline-sioux.html
	• Treaties Still Matter: The Dakota Access Pipeline: https://americanindian.si.edu/nk360/plains-treaties/dapl
	• Images
	  ○ Standing Rock: https://www.google.com/search?source=univ&tbm=isch&q=standing-rock&sa=X&ved=2ahUKEwiY3tjgtKfqAhXWK80KHezDDxUQsAR6BAgEFAE&biw=1536&bih=754&dpr=1.25
	  ○ Colonialism: https://www.google.com/search?q=colonialism&tbm=isch&ved=2ahUKEwiy05OXxuHqAhUJOa0KHZZVDRMQ2-cCegQIABAA&oq=colonialism&gs_lcp=CgNpbWcQAzIFCAAQsQMyAggAMgIIADICCAAyAggAMgIIADICCAAyAggAMgIIADICCAA6BAgAEEM6BwgAELEDEEM6CAgAELEDEIMBUJaiA1iYyANgiMsDaABwAHgCgAF3iAGaD5IBBDIwLjOYAQCgAQCgAQtnd3Mtd2l6LWltZ7ABAMABAQ&sclient=img&ei=Wo0YX7k-KYnytAWWq7WVAQ&bih=754&biw=1536

(Continued)

Table 1.1 Unit Overview and General Teaching Ideas *(Continued)*

• CCSS.ELA-LITERACY.RI.5.8
Explain how an author uses reasons and evidence to support particular points in a text, identifying which reasons and evidence support which point(s).
• CCSS.ELA-LITERACY.RI.5.9
Integrate information from several texts on the same topic in order to write or speak about the subject knowledgeably.
	• Tudor, A., Tudor, K. & Eaglespeaker, J. (2018). *Young water protectors: A story about standing rock.* CreateSpace Independent Publishing Platform.
	• Websites for Recommended Native American Books:
	  ○ Native American Children's Literature Recommended Reading List: https://www.firstnations.org/wp-content/uploads/2018/11/Revised_Book_Insert_Web_Version_March_2018.pdf
	  ○ Twenty #ownvoices Children's Books About Native Americans and First Nations Canadians: https://www.rebekahgienapp.com/native-americans/
	  ○ American Indians in Children's Literature: https://americanindiansinchildrensliterature.blogspot.com/p/best-books.html
	  ○ 32 Native American Children's Books: https://coloursofus.com/32-native-american-childrens-books/
	  ○ Native American Heritage Month: https://www.lapl.org/kids/books/native-american-heritage-month-childrens-book-book-list
	  ○ The Open Book Blog: https://blog.leeandlow.com/2017/11/20/native-american-heritage-month-our-favorite-childrens-books-by-native-authors/
	• Mount Rushmore: https://www.pbs.org/wgbh/americanexperience/features/rushmore-sioux/
	• Native Tribes Could Lose Federal Recognition of Tribal Sovereignty Under Trump: https://www.teenvogue.com/story/native-tribes-could-lose-federal-recognition-of-tribal-sovereignty-under-trump
	• How U.S. Gov't Is Helping Corporations Steal Native Land: http://inthesetimes.com/features/native-land-plunder-bureau-of-indian-affairs.html

Week Four

• History of the Southwestern and Western United States and Its People in Relation to Internal Colonialism
  ○ Expanding view to Indigenous groups in other continents

Colonialism and Native American Resiliency

Common Core Standards	Some Related Texts/Resources
• CCSS.ELA-LITERACY.RI.5.1 Quote accurately from a text when explaining what the text says explicitly and when drawing inferences from the text. • CCSS.ELA-LITERACY.RI.5.2 Determine two or more main ideas of a text and explain how they are supported by key details; summarize the text. • CCSS.ELA-LITERACY.RI.5.3 Explain the relationships or interactions between two or more individuals, events, ideas, or concepts in a historical, scientific, or technical text based on specific information in the text. • CCSS.ELA-LITERACY.RI.5.5 Compare and contrast the overall structure (e.g., chronology, comparison, cause/effect, problem/solution) of events, ideas, concepts, or information in two or more texts. • CCSS.ELA-LITERACY.RI.5.6 Analyze multiple accounts of the same event or topic, noting important similarities and differences in the point of view they represent. • CCSS.ELA-LITERACY.RI.5.7 Draw on information from multiple print or digital sources, demonstrating the ability to quickly locate an answer to a question or to solve a problem efficiently. • CCSS.ELA-LITERACY.RI.5.8 Explain how an author uses reasons and evidence to support particular points in a text, identifying which reasons and evidence support which point(s). • CCSS.ELA-LITERACY.RI.5.9 Integrate information from several texts on the same topic in order to write or speak about the subject knowledgeably.	• Oklahoma: https://www.okhistory.org/publications/encyclopediaonline and https://www.britannica.com/place/Oklahoma-state/History • W.O.W. Internal Colonialism: https://www.youtube.com/watch?v=49lxXuosx_k • Opinion: Half the Land in Oklahoma Could be Returned to Native Americans: https://newsela.com/read/lib-opinion-oklahoma-land-cherokee/id/56040?collection_id=339&search_id=7bc97209-772a-4b2c-b43b-bc52f010e95c • Justices Rule Swath of Oklahoma Remains Tribal Reservation: https://newsela.com/read/oklahoma-ruled-tribal-reservation/id/2001010980/?search_id=f1e6bda7-f88f-4781-b0d0-ddc083bea8f4 • The Word Indigenous Explained https://www.youtube.com/watch?v=ClSeEFTsgDA

2. Allow time for the groups/partners to read the article and then have them discuss the following questions: Does colonialism still exist? How has colonialism been justified in the past? What effects do we see now?
3. Walk around the room and monitor conversations and take anecdotal notes of student responses to use as an informal assessment to inform instructional next steps.
4. After the partner/small group discussion, have each student write an individual response to each of the questions in their reading journals or use it as an exit ticket. Written responses should be used as informal assessments to inform the next instructional steps.

Regroup

1. Ask the class to consider this question: "Does colonialism still exist today?" Give the students time to think silently and write a response in their journals. Then, have the class form a single line in the front of the room according to their response. Place a sign at one end of the classroom for "yes" and a sign at the other end of the classroom for "no." Put a sign for "maybe" in the middle to help students form one line that represents a continuum of their personal response to the question. Then, fold the student line in half. Take one end of the student line and have them become partners so the farthest "yes" is paired with the farthest "no."
2. Have one side talk first and give two minutes for them to share their response and then switch.
3. Remind students to respectfully listen to their partner's answer.

Use the individual exit ticket responses as an informal assessment.

Accommodations

- The article can be read aloud online to students and the reading level can be adjusted up or down.
- Key vocabulary in the article (e.g., greed, enslaved, and exclusion) can be pre-taught with students as needed.
- Students can have the opportunity to type or give verbal arguments for the writing prompts.
- Emergent bilinguals can respond in their First language. A peer or translator app can help relay the message.
- Sentence stems for writing or speaking:
  ○ A reason that colonialism has been justified in the past is _____.

- An example of how colonialism is seen today is _____.
- I agree with that point and would like to add _____.
- I disagree with that point. What about _____?

Sample Lesson Two: Internal Colonialism

Whole Group

1. Start the lesson by watching the video: *W.O.W. Internal Colonialism*: https://www.youtube.com/watch?v=49lxXuosx_k.
2. Next, have the class turn and talk to an elbow partner about examples of internal colonialism from U.S. history (e.g., Trail of Tears, inner-city ghettos, and red-lining). Then show the webpage, *History of Oklahoma: Encyclopedia Britannica*: https://www.britannica.com/place/Oklahoma-state/History or *The Oklahoma Historical Society*: https://www.okhistory.org/publications/encyclopediaonline, and discuss the history of Oklahoma and how it has affected all its people (Indigenous and White).
3. Next, show the webpage, *Uprooted: The 1950's Plan to Erase Indian Country*: apmreports.org, and listen to an excerpt about the experiences of Native Americans. Optional video: *The Word Indigenous Explained* from youtube.com

Small Group

1. Have the students read the Newsela article, *Opinion: Half the land in Oklahoma Could Be Returned to Native Americans*, and discuss the central idea and two supporting details.
2. How are Native Americans reacting to U.S. land policies? How should land ownership/rights be determined? What other connections with land stealing can you make?

Regroup

1. After they are finished, ask for volunteers to share what they wrote.
2. Share by showing on the screen or reading aloud the Newsela article *Justices Rule Swath of Oklahoma Remains Tribal Reservation*.

Informal Assessment

Use the exit ticket: Do you agree with the justices' decision? Why or why not? Include at least five supporting details for your argument.

Accommodations

- The article can be read aloud online to students and the reading level can be adjusted up or down.
- Key vocabulary in the article (e.g., ancestral, allotment, and jurisdiction) can be pre-taught to students as needed.
- Students can have options to type or give verbal arguments for the writing prompts.
- Emergent bilinguals can respond in their first language. A peer or translator app can help relay the message.
- Sentence stems for writing or speaking:
  - I think that land ownership should be determined by _____.
  - A connection I have with land stealing is in the country of _____ where _____ is happening.
  - I agree with that point and would like to add _____.
  - I disagree with that point. What about _____?

Extension Activity

Allow students to express their learning about colonialism in this unit through poetry. You can find many poetry templates at ReadWriteThink.org, such as shape, name, and theme poems. However, some students prefer to have more freedom of expression. The 5th grade student work sample in Figure 1.4 shows her original poem composed in response to her learning in this unit.

Imagination

Imagine owning something people compete for
Even if it's clearly yours
Imagine greeting someone with respect
But they treat you like a threat
Imagine getting slaughtered like pigs
But after the torment your tormentor moves on
Imagine getting killed because you didn't act like pawn
But frankly a lot of Native Americans didn't have to image that because of this happened to them and worse.

Figure 1.4 Imagination. *Michelle Abba.*

Guidelines for Student Individual Inquiry Project

Students will complete the culminating project explained at the end of the unit where they will have covered all of the criteria and details during the unit of a

Table 1.2 Indigenous People Group Student Inquiry Project Rubric

Criteria	Details	Points
Conventions	• Formatting • Neatness • Spelling and grammar	10
Research	• Historical and current land ownership • Creation story • Cultural traditions • Current social issues and how to support them	50

Resources	• Minimum four sources
	   ◦ Two must be authentic sources
	   ◦ Citations
		20

Presentation of Research	• 2–3 minutes • Clear mode of data visual ◦ Poster, PowerPoint, diorama, etc.	20

specific Native American group. For example, students will have had experience understanding that creation stories vary among different groups. They will know that land boundaries continue to change due to colonization. They will also know how to discern authentic and multiple perspective resources.

The purpose of the last lessons in week 4 of the unit is to help students realize that colonization is not unique to the United States and that Native Americans are not the only group to have been oppressed. To complete the project, students will have the freedom to choose to research any Indigenous group in the world—including additional groups from the United States.

Students will be given a week to complete this project. They will choose an Indigenous group and research an aspect of this group, such as cultural traditions or current social issues and how to support these people. Then they will choose a presentation mode for their findings (e.g., poster or PowerPoint). Presentations can be peer-evaluated and/or teacher-graded.

SUPPORT FOR EMERGENT BILINGUALS

- Multiple language opportunities
    - Translating: peer to peer, peer to teacher, etc.
    - Translanguaging: use of L1 for partner discussions and brainstorming with presentations in English or bilingual presentations
    - Array of texts in various languages
    - Newsela offers various articles in Spanish
- Use of visuals
    - Image examples for Stand Rock and Colonialism are provided in this chapter

- The articles and videos also provide image support
- Peer support
  - Partner reading
  - Partner editing for writing
  - Allow partners to brainstorm and plan in L1
- Sentence stems
  - I believe the land in Oklahoma should be returned to the Native Americans because _____.
- Audio of readings
  - Newsela provides a read-aloud option

SUPPORT FOR STUDENTS WITH SPECIAL LEARNING NEEDS

- Listening to the articles on the computer
  - Newsela offers a read-aloud option
- Typing, dictating, or using oral responses to questions
- Permitting students to work individually, with a partner, or small group
- Frequent breaks
- Present instructions orally and in writing
- Extended time to complete assignments
- Preferential seating
  - Allow the student to sit closer to you, the board, or near a peer support partner
- Provide space for minimal distractions
  - Allow the student to have a space away from distractions from other students or classroom displays
- Provide on-task/focusing prompts
  - Have a predetermined discrete signal (i.e., walk behind/in front of student's desk) that redirects the student back to the task

SUGGESTED MODIFICATIONS FOR OLDER ADOLESCENTS

This unit focused on early adolescents, specifically 5th grade, illustrating how justice and activism can be a part of learning, even in elementary school. However, teaching about Native American Resilience is appropriate for high school as well. Below are suggested modifications to teach this unit with older students.

- Select texts with a higher reading level and a more mature treatment of the content. Appropriate works of fiction have been included in the multimodal text set. For nonfiction, use reference articles appropriate for higher grades. For example, Britannica High School is a an excellent resources with built-in support for different readers. Additionally, Gale in Context (High School) and Infobase American History are appropriate for older students.
- Expand written responses to full essays, particularly an expository essay where students express an opinion on a modern-day event such as the #NotYourMascot campaign.
- Individual student projects can include a nuanced compare and contrast component for particular Indigenous groups.

REFERENCES

Bronner, S. (2018). Colonialism. *Encyclopedia of American studies.* Johns Hopkins University Press. https://search-credoreference-com.ezp.twu.edu/content/title/jhueas?institutionId=2115&tab=contents

Eagle Shield, A., Django, P., Paris, R., & San Pedro, T. (Eds.). (2020). *Education in movement spaces: Standing rock to Chicago freedom square.* Routledge.

Giorgis, C., & Johnson, N. J. (2002). Text sets. *Reading Teacher, 56*(2), 200–208. http://search.ebscohost.com.ezp.twu.edu/login.aspx?direct=true&db=eric&AN=EJ655270&site=ehost-live

Kumar, A. (2020). Why a former Olympic site is finally removing this Native American slur from its name. https://www.espn.com/olympics/story/_/id/29938592/why-former-olympic-site-removed-native-american-slur-women-name

Webster's (1989). *Webster's encyclopedic unabridged dictionary of the English language.* Random House Value Publishing.

Chapter 2

Modern-Day Colonialism

Washington D.C., Puerto Rico, and Other U.S. Territories

Marlene Walker

Figure 2.1 Puerto Rico Flag. *Joaquin Vargas.*

THEME AND RATIONALE

Understanding the citizenship status of people in Washington, D.C., Puerto Rico, and U.S. territories is essential if we are to reconstruct a society in the

United States as one embracing multiculturalism and decolonization. Too often, citizens of U.S. territories are treated as foreigners and, along with residents of Washington, D.C., denied representation in the government, which determines the circumstances of their lives. Many U.S. citizens are unaware of and, by extension, not empathetic toward issues surrounding Washington, D.C., Puerto Rico, and other U.S. territories. This lack of awareness results in denials of rights and ultimately rejection, prejudice, and oppression, leading to modern colonialism (Dropp & Nyhan, 2017). Nevertheless, these cycles of ignorance, colonization, and oppression are largely unexamined on a national scale.

Consider the U.S. territory of Puerto Rico. After the Spanish–American War in 1898, Spain ceded the island of Puerto Rico to the United States. Increasingly since then, the presence of Puerto Ricans in the mainland has remained strong for years on end. These U.S. citizens have fought in World War I (WWI) and World War II (WWII), and continue to serve in the military in great measure. More Puerto Ricans—around 5.4 million—now live in the United States than on the island of Puerto Rico, around 3.3 million (Caban, 2018). Fifty-four percent of U.S. citizens are not cognizant of the history of the oldest colony of the mainland and thus, do not understand the relationship between the two governmental bodies (Dropp & Nyhan, 2017).

In addition to Puerto Rico, the U.S. controls four other inhabited territories: Guam, American Samoa, the Northern Mariana Islands, and the U.S. Virgin Islands. The inhabitants of these territories do not have voting representatives in the U.S. Senate or House of Representatives, the same as the citizens of Washington, D.C. The latest population estimates put more than 700,000 people in Washington, D.C. (United States Census Bureau, 2019). For comparison, the same report by the U.S. Census (2019) puts the population of Wyoming at less than 580,000 people. The U.S. citizens in Washington, D.C., should not have less representation than the U.S. citizens in Wyoming. Additionally, the citizens of U.S. territories should have representation in the system which determines their standard of and circumstance in life.

As we continue to construct a future of improved relationships between the different cultures and races, which compose the fabric of the United States, it is important to understand that educators can begin to plant the seeds to bring about a much-needed unity. However, this unity will first require teaching history from multiple perspectives while informing students of the different rights and representations that various U.S. citizens possess.

Gloria Anzaldúa (1987) said in her book *Borderlands*:

> Like all people, we perceive the version of reality that our culture communicates. Like others having or living in more than one culture, we get multiple,

often opposing messages. The coming together of two self-consistent but habitually incomparable frames of reference causes un choque, a cultural collision. (p. 85)

Citizens from U.S. territories have experienced this "choque" Anzaldúa (1987) discusses, and continue to receive it each time they are treated as *extranjeros* or foreigners. This friction is evident when examining political issues of U.S. territories: choosing status quo, statehood, or independence. These issues are often ignored by the U.S. government and rarely included in instruction, producing new generations of citizens who lack basic and nuanced knowledge on this timely issue.

For example, this particular topic is not covered in the current social studies/history Common Core State Standards (CCSS), thus giving a one-sided perspective: the dominant culture's. The unit presented here implements standards and skills from many curricular areas such as language arts, history, government, citizenship, culture, and social studies. Pertinent CCSS that relate to the lessons in this unit are explicitly provided in the unit overview.

UNIT GOALS

This unit will allow students to familiarize themselves with what commonwealths, territories, and districts are and the benefits, as well as the disadvantages, of those relationships among countries. The unit is designed for adolescents in grades 6 through 8 but includes adaptations for both younger and older adolescents. Students will explore the history of U.S. territories and Washington, D.C., as they relate to the United States as commonwealths, territories, and districts. Additionally, students will analyze ideas surrounding citizenship and democratic representation. The teacher and students accomplish this exploration and analysis through the use of multimodal resources including authentic literature from the marginalized communities discussed in this unit.

MULTIMODAL TEXT SET

The unit and lessons are intended to be applied from a critical stance, giving students the opportunity to decide how the dynamics of power in history explain decisions taken by the people in power, and how these decisions perpetuate dominance over the oppressed. The text set includes literature that exemplifies the conditions and feelings of individuals from the time of their colonization all the way to the present. Additionally, classrooms that will use this text set are likely multicultural and multilingual learning spaces which is the reality of today's U.S. schools. Therefore, the text set includes different perspectives, cultural representations, and languages in addition to modalities. The purpose of a multimodal curriculum is to offer students multiple ways to learn while interacting with text and various methods to express their learning through reader response. Consequently, many texts are in Spanish and most of them can be adapted to various languages which the author strongly suggests, even if you are teaching in an English-medium classroom. Like Freire and Macedo (1987) tell us, "Literacy can only be emancipatory and critical to the extent that it is conducted in the language of the people" (p. 159).

Books

- Charles, T. (2021). *Freedom Soup*. Candlewick.
- de Burgos, J. (1997). *Song of the simple truth: The complete poems of Julia de Burgos*. Curbstone Books.
- Denise, A. (2019). *Planting Stories: The life of librarian and storyteller Pura Belpre*. Harper, an imprint of HarperCollins.
- Diaz, J. (2018). *Islandborn*. Dial Books for Young Readers.
- Laguerre, E. (1975). *La Resaca*. Editorial Cultural, Inc.
- Marques, R. (1983). *La carreta*. Editorial Cultural.
- Newlevant, H. (2018). *Puerto Rico strong*. Oni Press.
- Rivera, L. (2020). *Never look back*. Bloomsbury Children's Books.
- Roth, S. L., & Trumbore, C. (2013). Parrots over Puerto Rico. Lee & Low Books, Inc.
- Santiago, E. (2006). *When I was Puerto Rican*. Da Capo.
- Zeno Gandía, M. (2013). *La charca*. CreateSpace Independent Publishing Platform.

Videos

- Speech Call to independence/Discurso de Albizu Campos (grito de Lares). https://www.youtube.com/watch?v=Y9z2Uwh9rfY
- Overview of the U.S. and PR relationship video, three parts. https://www.youtube.com/watch?v=NP5Jcvke_es
- Why Puerto Rico is not a U.S. state. https://www.youtube.com/watch?v=8EOxtY3M6Co
- Descubriendo Puerto Rico. https://fb.watch/51rbKJUGyw/
- The fifty-five states of America: U.S. Territories Explained. https://www.youtube.com/watch?v=nDxinFjlVmo

- Territories of the USA (Geography Now!) https://www.youtube.com/watch?v=5v0Ppl1B_wQ
- How the United States leaves behind its own American territories. https://www.youtube.com/watch?v=luiZZmZYOA8
- Washington, D.C.—The fight for America's 51st state, explained. https://www.youtube.com/watch?v=bfUeekXbYzk
- Guam: Why America's most isolated territory exists. https://www.youtube.com/watch?v=5r90DYjZ76g
- American Samoa: American forgotten colonies part 1. https://www.youtube.com/watch?v=9vit2Myiwro

Websites

- National Anthem Orchestra—La Boriqueña Lyrics. https://www.hymne-national.com/en/national-anthem-puerto-rico/
- Literatura Puertorriqueña. https://www.slideshare.net/MariaPetrovitch/literatura-puertorriquea
- Poem: Río Grande de Loíza. http://www.elboricua.com/Poems_Burgos_RioGrandeLoiza.html
- Memorias. Revista Digital de Historia y Arqueología desde el Caribe. https://www.redalyc.org/revista.oa?id=855

Articles

- Bigelow, B. (2018). We know Columbus landed in the Caribbean, but what of the people there? *Newsela.com*.
- Byrne, A. (2017). Yes, the U.S. had an empire—and in the Virgin Islands, it still does. *Newsela.com*.
- Cabán, P. (2018). Puerto Rico's forever exodus. *NACLA*. https://nacla.org/news/2018/02/22/puerto-rico's-forever-exodus
- Garcia, M. (2018). Julia de Burgos, una poetisa que ayudó a moldear la identidad puertorriqueña. *New York Times*.
- Kiddle (2021). History of Puerto Rico facts for kids. *Kiddle*. https://nacla.org/news/2018/02/22/puerto-rico%E2%80%99s-forever-exodus
- Newsela (2020). Primary source: Spain gives up control of Philippines, Puerto Rico, and Cuba. *Newsela.com*.
- *New York Times* (2016). Time machine (1898): U.S. begins the invasion of Puerto Rico. *Newsela.com*.
- Rivera, M. G., & Lopez, L. A. O. (2018). El español y el inglés en Puerto Rico: Una polémica de más de un siglo. *CENTRO: Journal of the Center for Puerto Rican Studies, 30(1)*, 106+.

- ThoughtCo.com (2019). What is the difference between a commonwealth and a state? *Newsela.com.*
- *Washington Post* (2018). Comic books provide quite a relief for Puerto Rican hurricane victims. *Newsela.com.*

SAMPLE LESSONS

Teachers may choose to use the text set to create a variety of lessons that cover the ideas outlined in Table 2.1. The sample lessons below represent some of those possibilities.

Sample Lesson 1: The Spanish–American War and the Resulting Commonwealths

Content Objective: The student will research on the Spanish–American War and its results, including the victor and the measures taken to reach peace.

Language Objective: Students will listen to and read different resources provided by the teacher but also include self-found information from the web, and will present their findings orally and in writing.

Key Vocabulary: Spanish–American War, commonwealth, colonialism, Treaty of Paris, Jones–Shafroth Act

Materials:
- List of terms for the scavenger hunt (handout or visibly displayed)
- List of preferred resources for students to use (select three to five from the text set as well as some in Spanish)
- Computers with Google Slides (preferred for group work) or PowerPoint

Procedure:
1. Read the objectives and ask students to explain to each other what those might mean.
2. Activate prior knowledge: Ask students if any of them have heard about the Spanish–American War or the U.S. territories. Then, ask them what usually happens after a war. Have them answer the questions with their partner or table (turn and talk). Then, ask a couple of students to share their thoughts with the whole class.
3. Tell the students that they will be participating in a scavenger hunt so they can find out information about the Spanish–American War.
4. Provide them a list of the terms they need to find which might include Spanish–American War, commonwealth, colonialism, Treaty of Paris,

Table 2.1 Unit Overview and General Teaching Ideas

Week One
- Spanish–American War
- What is a commonwealth? The different territories of the United States.
- Pros and cons of commonwealth relationships

Common Core Standards	Some Related Texts
• CCSS.ELA-LITERACY.RH.6-8.1 Cite specific textual evidence to support analysis of primary and secondary sources. • CCSS.ELA-LITERACY.RH.6-8.2 Determine the central ideas or information of a primary or secondary source; provide an accurate summary of the source distinct from prior knowledge or opinions. • CCSS.ELA-LITERACY.RH.6-8.4 Determine the meaning of words and phrases as they are used in a text, including vocabulary specific to domains related to history/social studies.	• Newsela (2020). Primary source: Spain gives up control of Philippines, Puerto Rico, and Cuba. *Newsela.com*. • *New York Times* (2016). Time machine (1898): U.S. begins the invasion of Puerto Rico. *Newsela.com*. • The fifty-five states of America: U.S. Territories Explained. https://www.youtube.com/watch?v=nDxinFjlVmo.

Week Two
- The case of Puerto Rico
- Relating history to current events
  - Hurricane Maria, its effects, and the U.S. response

Common Core Standards	Some Related Texts
• CCSS.ELA-LITERACY.RH.6-8 Integrate visual information (e.g., in charts, graphs, photographs, videos, or maps) with other information in print and digital texts.	• Rivera, L. (2020). *Never look back*. Bloomsbury Children's Books.

Week Three
- Literature and arts that reflect Puerto Rican feelings about the political situation
- Author Studies
  - Julia De Burgos
  - Pedro Albizu Campos
  - Lola Rodriguez de Tio

Common Core Standards	Some Related Texts
• CCSS.ELA-LITERACY.RH.6-8.10 By the end of grade 8, read and comprehend history/social studies texts in grades 6–8 text complexity band independently and proficiently.	• de Burgos, J. (1997). *Song of the simple truth: The complete poems of Julia de Burgos*. Curbstone Books. • Garcia, M. (2018). Julia de Burgos, una poetisa que ayudó a moldear la identidad puertorriqueña. *New York Times*.

Enrichment and Extension
- Washington, D.C.
- American Samoa
- Guam
- U.S. Virgin Islands

Jones–Shafroth Act, and other terms you select from the reading/viewing you will provide them.
5. Share the resources that you select from the text set above. Explain that they will receive extra points if they find information from the point of view of the Spaniards or other groups involved.
6. Ask students to begin a collaborative PowerPoint of their findings where they can add different resources including pictures, maps, and diagrams to explain the terms that they find.
7. Divide the class into academically and linguistically heterogeneous groups.
8. Provide Spanish resources and encourage Spanish-speaking students to use their language skills to enrich their findings.
9. Give students a set amount of time to do the scavenger hunt such as a class period.
10. Students share their findings through a presentation. As the students share, have other groups check, and add missing information that is being shared to their projects. Table 2.2 provides a rubric that students can use to self-evaluate their participation in this project.

Extension Activities:
- Students can write a script that portrays how the people involved in the events may have felt from the point of view of a person who was male, female, young, old, a child, rich, or poor.
- Students can make a poster representing the events of the Spanish–American War and present the poster to another person or group.

Sample Lesson 2: Hurricane Maria

Content Objective: The student will continue building knowledge on what a Commonwealth is by examining Puerto Rico during and after Hurricane Maria.

Language Objective: The student will listen and read different resources in English and Spanish related to Hurricane Maria, relief efforts, and will evaluate the events through a social justice lens. The student will then present their findings and viewpoints orally and in writing.

Key Vocabulary: commonwealth, citizenship, territory, social justice, culture, FEMA, Hurricane Maria, Hurricane Harvey

Materials:
- Computers or technology with Internet access
- Comic anthology book: *Puerto Rico Strong* (2018)

Table 2.2 Group Project Self-Evaluation Rubric

	Content	Organization	Resources	Writing Conventions		Learning
Needs revision	1 I included some information about the topic, but I did not expand on ideas.	1 I posted information on the slides, but my ideas were not organized.	1 I used one resource.	1 My writing was not clear or appropriate for the audience.	1	I cannot explain what I learned to a classmate.
Competent	2 I included one or two details about the topic.	2 The order of the slides is organized by subtitles.	2 I used two resources.	2 My writing was understandable, but had many errors.	2	I can explain one piece of information to others.
Good	3 I included all information requested.	3 The order of the subtitles makes sense.	3 I used three resources.	3 I used correct use of conventions such as punctuation, capitalization, grammar, and spelling.	3	I can give a general explanation of the topic.
Outstanding	4 I included all information requested and found some more.	4 I can explain why the group chose the order in which our ideas were presented.	4 I used three or more resources in more than one language.	4 I used conventions in an excellent way such as punctuation, capitalization, grammar, and spelling.	4	I can give explanations about the topic and specific details in one language or more.

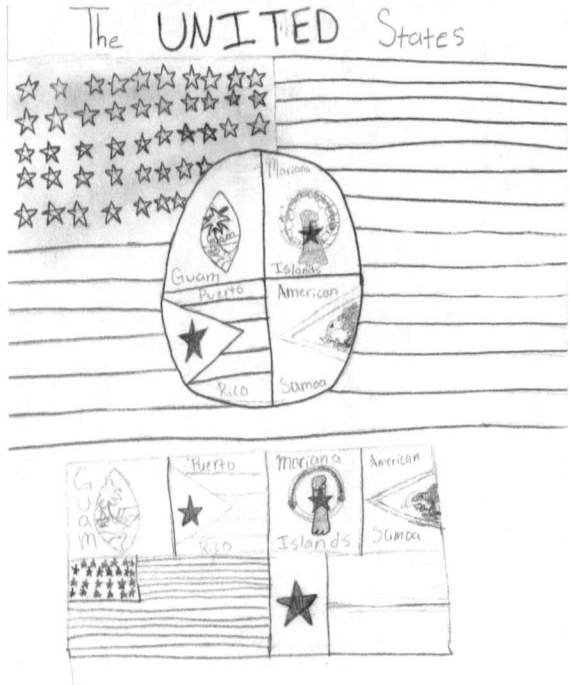

Figure 2.2 **The UNITED States.** *Mariana Estrada.*

- Newsela article: "Comics creators unite to help hurricane victims in Puerto Rico"
- Nearpod collaboration board set up for student "exit ticket" and with the code ready.

Procedures:
- Read the objectives and ask students to explain to each other what those might mean.
- Activate prior knowledge: Ask students if they remember when Houston was hit by Hurricane Harvey and what the news on T.V. showed about this hurricane. Do they know someone who was affected by Hurricane Harvey? Have students share their thoughts. Ask students if they heard about Hurricane Maria, which occurred about the same time, and how it devastated Puerto Rico. Remind students that Puerto Rico is a territory of the United States and that they will compare and contrast the relief responses of Hurricane Harvey in the United States and Hurricane Maria in Puerto Rico.
- Provide each student the Newsela article on Hurricane Maria. Read the article through shared reading, stopping at certain points to clarify information.

As you read aloud, the students follow along on their own hard or digital copies of the article.
- Divide students into small heterogeneous groups (academically and linguistically).
- Each student within the group will search for newspaper articles that discuss both the hurricanes, the effects, and FEMA's responses. They can also include information about politics surrounding the hurricanes if relevant.
- Provide students access to relevant websites where they might find this information such as Newsela and NewsForKids. You can also include local news outlets as well as national media such as CNN.
- Provide students with a graphic organizer where they write down the news source and then take notes on the effects and FEMA's response to both Hurricane Harvey and Hurricane Maria. Students can also create this graphic organizer in their notebooks.
- Allow time for reading and discussion within the group so they can synthesize the information. This time will be used to have each individual student take a stand about whether the actions or lack thereof were justified or not. To review Puerto Rican history from a Puerto Rican perspective, students can read the comic *Puerto Rico Strong* (2018), an anthology of various comics. Students can revisit any resources used in previous lessons.
- Divide the whole class into two groups based on the response to Hurricane Maria: response was appropriate versus response was not appropriate. Allow students to individually explain their thinking backed up with evidence from resources used so far in the whole unit in writing. Make sure students understand that oftentimes the media may be biased and that they have to be good judges of what they read.
- Have each group take turns presenting (one person from one group shares one thing and then another person from the other group shares, and so on).
- Have students evaluate their experience doing this exercise and share using a program such as Nearpod Collaborate Board or a Google Jamboard.

Extension Activities:
- Students can write a poem, song, or comic about ideas on how Puerto Ricans can become an accepted group within the United States.
- Students can use the resources in the text set to learn about other territories and commonwealths in the United States. Then, students can share their learning through the modality of their choice. Figure 2.2 is a 5th grade student's artwork that illustrates her understanding of U.S. territories and commonwealths.

GUIDELINES FOR A STUDENT INDIVIDUAL INQUIRY PROJECT

If educators are to include multiple perspectives in their teaching and make it the norm in schools, the need to begin exposing student from a very young age to all those perspectives. In this unit, students can learn about different perspectives by interviewing people from Puerto Rico. To do this, reach out to the Hispanic Chamber of Commerce, community centers, your school, and most importantly, parents and family members of your students. Identify people from Puerto Rico that your students can interview individually. If that is not possible, locate one or two people for the whole class to interview in person or through an online platform. Preferably, students can individually conduct interviews with Puerto Ricans of different ages to ask about their views on the political status of the island, how they learned about their history, and their identity. After conducting the interviews, students can present their learning through a presentation, using at least two modalities such as text and images.

SUPPORT FOR EMERGENT BILINGUALS

Because of the multilingual/multicultural lens adopted, which should be the norm, examples of how to accommodate emergent bilinguals are embedded in every decision of the lessons. The heterogeneous groupings, encouraging of the use of translanguaging, and using resources in the different languages represented in the class, are all a must.

- Scavenger Hunt: Pair students new to the country or emergent bilinguals with a student who speaks their language. Provide them resources in their language to conduct research so they can participate in a meaningful way.
- Encourage Spanish-speaking students, especially emergent bilinguals, to use their Spanish language skills to conduct research about Puerto Rico. Encourage them to present their research in Spanish or bilingually.
- Allow for the use of translanguaging to communicate in all domains: listening, speaking, reading, and writing. Use this instructional approach intentionally and strategically.

SUPPORT FOR STUDENTS WITH SPECIAL LEARNING NEEDS

Students with special needs will also benefit from many of the same supports for emergent bilinguals. Additionally, consider the following ways to create a more inclusive classroom during this unit.

- Allow for the use of technology, such as voice to text and higher percentage viewing, when conducting the research.
- Break the lessons and inquiry projects into smaller chunks for students to complete. Encourage students to work at the pace that allows them to participate in meaningful learning.
- Consider putting some students in a smaller group supported by a teacher assistant for the group work and inquiry project.

TEACHING A MODIFIED UNIT FOR ELEMENTARY OR HIGH SCHOOL STUDENTS

Although this unit is designed for middle school students, the content may be adapted for both upper elementary and high school students. To use in the 4th or 5th grade, the educator can use the lowest Lexile level for articles in Newsela and the picture books recommended. A good option for younger students is the Kiddle article in the multimodal text set. Since many of these concepts are abstract, the elementary educator can focus on fewer of them during the unit. For students in high school, the resources shared in this text set are appropriate. Some resources may include more difficult text and vocabulary that would be more appropriate for older, high school–aged students.

REFERENCES

Anzaldúa, G. (1987). *Borderlands/La frontera: The new mestiza.* Aunt Lute Books.

Caban, P. (2017). Puerto Ricans as contingent citizens: Shifting mandated identities and imperial disjunctures. *Centro Journal, 29*(1), 238–283.

Dropp, K., & Nyhan, B. (2017, September 26). Nearly half of Americans don't know Puerto Ricans are fellow citizens. *The New York Times: Upshot.* https://www.nytimes.com/2017/09/26/upshot/nearly-half-of-americans-dont-know-people-in-puerto-ricoans-are-fellow-citizens.html

Freire, P., & Macedo, D. (1987). *Literacy: Reading the word and the world.* Bergin & Garvey.

United States Census Bureau. (2019). *2019 population estimates.* https://www.census.gov/search-results.html?searchType=web&cssp=SERP&q=population%20washington%20dc

Chapter 3

Immigration

The Fabric of Our Nation

Yismelle Duran

Figure 3.1 Unity. *Hazzbel Martinez.*

THEME AND RATIONALE

The diversity of the U.S. population is a product of the constant flow of immigration that has occurred from precolonial times to the present, and it is that diversity that has shaped this nation to become what it is. Despite the relevance of this phenomenon, the social studies curriculum implemented in most school districts does not treat this topic with the level of importance it deserves. Furthermore, most social studies textbooks do not have a specific unit on immigration. Rather, they embed the immigration topic into the different time periods that are included in the U.S. history curriculum.

However, immigration is not only numbers or the historical events that produce them. Immigration has a more important face, one that goes beyond textbooks, transactions, and paperwork. Behind every immigrant there is an important story, oftentimes ignored, that will tell you why people migrate and why the United States has been chosen as the desired destination. Immigration, defined as the act of immigrating, implies that people travel to a country with the purpose of establishing permanent residence in that country (Merriam-Webster Dictionary, n.d.). Notwithstanding, a considerable number of immigrants will tell you that they never intended to leave their home country. There were particular circumstances, including running for their lives, that pushed them to make that decision (Portes & Rumbaut, 2014).

Since its declaration of independence, this country has been described as a nation of immigrants and that is irrefutable. Literally, almost everyone in this country, except for Native Americans, is a descendant of an immigrant even if it is from many generations ago. The United States is one of the largest receivers of immigrants in the world and data from 2018 indicates that about 13.7 percent of the population was foreign-born (Pew Research Center, 2020).

The word immigration has a bad reputation, one that has been created and promoted by nationalist and xenophobic groups who might be afraid of the change that immigrants bring to a nation. Moreover, those in positions of power often use the media to manipulate this topic and produce reactions that alienate the population to oppose immigration. For example, when a politician uses derogatory speech to refer to an immigrant group, it automatically creates a sentiment of rejection toward that particular group and all immigrants in general, which sometimes is taken to lengths where people are discriminated against or abused based on their appearance, race, or ethnicity.

UNIT GOALS

Therefore, the purpose of this unit is to show the perspective of immigrants to provide students with a broader picture and better understanding of what drives immigration and how it affects both immigrants and the receiving nation. Students will explore immigration from both a historical and a modern perspective. Through this unit, both you and your students will develop a better understanding of the push and pull factors of immigration (Portes &

Rumbaut, 2014); what pushes people out of their countries and what pulls them to want to make the sacrifices for a chance of a better life. As a teacher, you might even develop an appreciation of the complex reasons many of your own students are sitting in your classroom (Stewart, 2017). Furthermore, although this unit is designed for 9th and 10th grade social studies, it is also applicable to the English language arts or world language classroom.

MULTIMODAL TEXT SET

This unit uses a set of multimodal texts to provide teachers and students multiple opportunities and resources to explore the topic of immigration on a local and global scale from the comfort of the classroom. It will allow teachers to engage students in experiences that go beyond reading a textbook chapter or an article. Students will have the opportunity to read, watch, and hear informational text, as well as experience immersing themselves in the Ellis Island immigration museum through a virtual reality (VR) video, and other different experiences that will transport them to a new environment. This approach adopts a critical literacy stance that gives educators the tools that will allow them to address the theme of immigration through the perspective of immigrants, and broaden the understanding of students on this particular issue.

The resources presented here are intended to support classroom exploration of the topic of immigration. Several of these texts are included in the sample lessons while additional resources are provided for individual student projects and flexibility. There are more applications of these texts than those presented in the sample lessons. For example, any of these resources could be used to initiate classroom discussion, introduce or close a lesson, or provide additional resources for students who are working ahead of schedule or would like to explore the issue further. Another possibility is providing selection opportunities of particular texts to different students, differentiating based on strengths and interests, and asking students to present their learning to the class or a group. Teachers can include a choice board of presentation options to reflect students' strengths and comfort. For example, some students may be comfortable speaking in front of groups and others would prefer to create a website to share their findings. As classroom experts, instructors should not feel limited to the suggested uses in this chapter.

Young Adult Novels

- Argueta, J. (2019). *Caravan to the North: Misael's long walk.* Groundwood Books.

- Bencastro, M. (1998). *Odyssey to the North*. Arte Publico Press.
- Brown, S. (2016). *Caminar*. Candlewick Press.
- Diaz, A. (2016). *The only road*. Simon & Schuster Books for Young Readers.
- Diaz, A. (2016). *El único destino*. Simon & Schuster Books for Young Readers.
- Diaz, A. (2018). *The crossroads*. Simon & Schuster.
- Diaz, A. (2020). *La travesía de Santiago*. Simon & Schuster Books for Young Readers.
- Engle, M. (2017). *Tropical secrets: Holocaust refugees in Cuba*. Henry Holt and Company LLC.
- Flores-Garbis, E. (2012). *90 miles to Havana*. Roaring Brook Press.
- Grande, R. (2013). *The distance between us*. Washington Square Press.
- Guerrero, D., & Burford, M. (2016). *En el país que amamos: Mi familia dividida*. Henry Holt and Company.
- Henriquez, C. (2014). *El libro de los Americanos desconocidos*. Una división de Random House LLC.
- Jimenez, F. (2002). *Senderos fronterizos: Breaking through*. Houghton Mifflin.
- Kullab, S., Roche, J., & Freiheit, M. (2017). *Escape from Syria*. Firefly Books.
- Latin American Youth Center. (2018). *Voces sin fronteras: Our stories, our truth*. Shout Mouse Press.
- Manuel, J., Pineda, C., Galisky, A., & Shine, R. (Eds.). (2012). *Papers: Stories by undocumented youth*. Graham Street Productions.
- Muñoz Ryan, P. (2002). *Esperanza rising*. Scholastic Inc.
- Orner, P. (Ed.). (2017). *Underground America: Narratives of undocumented lives (Voices of witness)*. Verso.
- Thorpe, H. (2009). *Just like us: The true story of four Mexican girls coming of age in America*. Simon & Schuster.
- Torres Sanchez, J. (2020). *We are not from here*. Philomel Books.
- Warga, J. (2019). *Other words for home*. Harper Collins Publishing.
- Wilson, T. (2016). *Through my eyes*. Beaver's Pond Press.

Essays

- Gallo, R. (Ed.). (2007). *First crossing: Stories about teen immigrants*. Candlewick Press.
- Thanh Nguyen, V. (Ed.). (2019). *Displaced: Refugee writers on refugee lives*. Abrams Press.

Poetry

- Ahmad, D. (Ed.). (2019). *The penguin book of migration literature: Departures, arrivals, generations, returns*. Penguin Books.

- Bowles, G. (2018). *They call me güero*. Whack Publications.
- Flor Ada, A. & Campoy, F. I. (2016). *Yes, we are Latinos: Poems and prose about the Latino experience*. Charlesbridge.
- Vecchione, P. & Raymond, A. (Ed.). (2019). *Ink knows no borders*. Seven Stories Press.

Children's Books

- Buitrago, J. & Yockteng, R. (2015). *Two white rabbits*. Groundwood Books.
- Del Rizzo, S. (2017). *My beautiful birds*. Pajama Press.
- Ringgold, F. (2016). *We came to America*. Alfred A. Knopf.
- Sanna, F. (2016). *The journey*. Flying Eye Books.
- Tonatiuh, D. (2014). *Separate is never equal: Sylvia Mendez and her family's fight for desegregation*. Abrams Books for Young Readers.
- Williams, K. L. & Mohammed, K. (2007). *Four feet, two sandals*. Eerdmans Books for Young Readers.
- Yaccarino, D. (2012). *All the way to America: The story of a big Italian family and a little shovel*. Random House LLC.

Documentaries

- Dissard, J. M. & Peng, G. (Directors). (2013). I learn America. [Film]. Dissard & Peng.

Paintings and Pictures

The images in Table 3.1 were found through a web search using "U.S. immigration art" as the search command.

Audio and Audiovisual Texts

Table 3.2 contains various audio and audiovisual texts accompanied by their description and the URL addresses to access them.

SAMPLE LESSONS

One of the main goals of teaching this unit is to bring the immigrants' voices to the discussion and thus analyze texts that will provide access to hearing their stories. Table 3.3 illustrates the unit's overview. The multimodal text set and the sample lessons, with additional resources, below will guide educators into teaching a more comprehensive and relevant immigration unit. After

Table 3.1 Paintings and Pictures to Investigate Immigration

Art Spiegelman's "A Warm Welcome," 2015	
Edel Rodrigue's "Strangers," 2018	
Alfredo Jaar's "Ellis Island, 2024," 2018, based on a photograph by Masahito Ono	
Felipe Baez's "Untitled (so much darkness, so much brownness)," 2016	
"Sueños Húmedos" ("Wet Dreams") by Juan Carlos Marcias	
Tatyana Fazlalizadeh's "Portrait of My Father as an Alien," 2018	

(Continued)

Table 3.1 Paintings and Pictures to Investigate Immigration (*Continued*)

The real stories of the superheroes by Dulce Pinzon.
Spiderman—Bernabe Mendez from the State of Guerrero works as a professional window cleaner in New York; he sends $500 a month.
Visit https://www.dulcepinzon.com/ for more pictures of this collection.

Children play in front of a new mural on the Mexican side of a border wall in Tijuana, Mexico, Friday, Aug. 9, 2019. The mural shows faces of people deported from the United States with barcodes that activate first-person narratives on visitors' phones.
Elliot Spagat, AP

Mexican National Guard Soldiers patrol the beach section of the Tijuana U.S.-Mexico Border Fence, in Tijuana, Mexico, Sunday, July 21, 2019.
Hans-Maximo Muselik, AP

Activists express their support for immigrants and refugees. (Nitish Meena)

each lesson is presented there are some general recommendations on how to present the lesson from the perspective of a high school teacher. Each of the sample lessons may also be in Spanish for a bilingual, Spanish language arts, or Spanish as a world language classroom.

Sample Lesson One: Introduction to Historical Immigration

In this multi-day lesson, students will gain a better understanding of U.S. immigration history, policy, and the different perceptions about this topic using multimodal texts. Start the lesson by providing an outline of all the activities that will be completed in class for each day. Then give instructions to students on how to complete the tasks in the timeline. It would be ideal to have the groups preselected before the class to save time. Display or set a timer on the board so students know how much time they have left as they work in the teams. While they work, walk around the classroom to check their work and provide guidance. Then, when they finish their boards and present, go ahead and introduce the next set of activities. Lastly, get ready for leading the discussion and pass out the sticky notes for the exit ticket as they finish reading the articles. Have the exit ticket question displayed on the board.

Student-Friendly Learning Targets:
- I can talk about the history of U.S. immigration naming specific time periods and events that produced major immigration waves, including the most recent ones.
- I can compare different perceptions on the topic of immigration and how they affect public opinion and policy considerations.

Duration of the Lesson: 90 minutes (two 45-minute class periods)
Materials: Classroom projector, computers with internet access, butcher or bulletin board paper, scissors, markers, sticky notes, VR goggles (optional)
Activities:
- **U.S. Immigration Timeline (35 Minutes)**

The class will be divided into eight small groups. Each group will be assigned a different immigration-related era that they will present to the whole class on a large paper that will be put together on the classroom wall as a timeline. In addition to the paper, students can use a digital presentation to illustrate their ideas or to display digital work such as pictures and videos. Students will mainly use the History Channel website to study their topic, which can be accessed using the following link: https://www.history.com/topics/immigration/immigration-united-states-timeline

Table 3.2 Audio and Audiovisual Teaching Resources on Immigration

Title of Resource	Description	Access
Only in America	This is a podcast in which church leaders, law enforcement officials, business owners, and others speak openly about the way culture, identity, and values are shaping and defining the country. They focus on offering a constructive way forward on immigration.	https://immigrationforum.org/landing_page/podcast/
U.S. Immigration | Let's Talk | NPR	For over 200 years the U.S. Immigration policies have determined who the United States lets in, and who is shut out. NPR's Tom Gjelten explains. NPR is an American public broadcast service.	https://www.youtube.com/watch?v=m9zf8hkCqIg
How Immigrants Shape(d) the United States | Nalini Krishnankutty | TEDxPSU—March 2, 2018	Do immigrants need the United States, or does the United States need its immigrants? Writer, researcher, and first-generation immigrant American Nalini Krishnankutty showcases many surprising examples of traditions, businesses, and ideas that are considered All-American today, but which owe their origins to first-generation immigrants.	https://www.youtube.com/watch?v=irtxoIPBVWs
What If You Were An Immigrant? | Ben Huh | TEDxPortland—June 2, 2013	In this moving TEDxPortland Talk, Ben discusses what it means to be an immigrant and the importance of policy and awareness of who we are letting in and why.	https://www.youtube.com/watch?v=Pi1TjE13S3s
Being a Refugee Is Not a Choice: Carina Hoang at TEDxPerth—January 15, 2014	Refugees are often marginalized; their humanity is ignored as their stories go untold. In this remarkable and emotional talk, however, author and former refugee Carina Hoang discusses her experience as a "boat person." It's a powerful account that is impossible to ignore.	https://www.youtube.com/watch?v=JwkVk16xecw
Fatoumata Diawara—Nterini	This is an excellent music video and song which shares the migrant experience.	https://youtu.be/4gmGL5SqhaY

The eight topics for the eight groups are:

1. White People of "Good Character" Granted Citizenship
2. Irish Immigrant Wave
3. Chinese Exclusion Act
4. Ellis Island Opens
5. New Restrictions at Start of WWI
6. Mexicans Fill Labor Shortages during WWII
7. Quota System Ends
8. Amnesty to Illegal Immigrants

- **Ellis Island 360 (VR Experience)**

As an extension activity as groups complete their timeline, and if resources are available (i.e., VR goggles), the teacher can offer students the opportunity to tour Ellis Island through the following YouTube video: https://www.youtube.com/watch?v=uUVpvbrRGYg

- **Policy: Types of Immigration Status (15 Minutes)**

Using the USDS Department of Consular Affairs website, students write their own definitions of the different immigration statuses. Immigrant categories: U.S. Department of State—Department of Consular Affairs:

- https://travel.state.gov/content/travel/en/us-visas/immigrate.html
- https://travel.state.gov/content/travel/en/us-visas/visa-information-resources/all-visa-categories.html

- **Understanding Immigration (15 Minutes)**

Students will read this opinion article from Newsela and respond to a set of reflection questions. Opinion: Why Is Immigration Different from Trade? https://newsela.com/read/election-2020-immigration-trade/id/2001004958/?collection_id=339&search_id=7fcce41a-e2c9-4ab8-bf4f-dae9659e8548

Questions for student reflection in the journals and/or through discussion:

1. How is immigration similar to trade according to the author?
2. How does the United States exemplify the benefits of immigration? Provide an example.
3. What are the risks of immigration?
4. What is the approach to immigration that the author suggests?

Table 3.3 Unit Overview and General Teaching Ideas

Weeks One–Two
- Historical migration to the United States

Common Core Standards	Some Related Texts
• Key Ideas and Details: • CCSS.ELA-LITERACY.RH.9-10.1 Cite specific textual evidence to support the analysis of primary and secondary sources, attending to such features as the date and origin of the information. • CCSS.ELA-LITERACY.RH.9-10.2 Determine the central ideas or information of a primary or secondary source; provide an accurate summary of how key events or ideas develop over the course of the text. • CCSS.ELA-LITERACY.RH.9-10.9 Compare and contrast treatments of the same topic in several primary and secondary sources. • Craft and Structure: • CCSS.ELA-LITERACY.RH.9-10.4 Determine the meaning of words and phrases as they are used in a text, including vocabulary describing political, social, or economic aspects of history/social science.	• NPR video on U.S. immigration • Articles about immigration from Newsela • *We Came to America* picture book • Poetry books in text set • Ellis Island website • How Immigrants Shape(d) the United States TED Talk • History channel website

Weeks Three–Five
- Modern Migration

Common Core Standards	Some Related Texts
• CCSS.ELA-LITERACY.RH.9-10.5 Analyze how a text uses structure to emphasize key points or advance an explanation or analysis. • CCSS.ELA-LITERACY.RH.9-10.6 Compare the point of view of two or more authors for how they treat the same or similar topics, including which details they include and emphasize in their respective accounts. • CCSS.ELA-LITERACY.RH.9-10.3 Analyze in detail a series of events described in a text; determine whether earlier events caused later ones or simply preceded them.	• *The Distance Between Us* (available in the original and YA version in both English and Spanish) • *The Only Road*. (available in English and Spanish) • Both books above have sequels for continued reading engagement on the topic • Artwork in the text set

Weeks Six–Seven
- Perspectives of Future Immigration Policies

Common Core Standards	Some Related Texts
• CCSS.ELA-LITERACY.RH.9-10.8 Assess the extent to which the reasoning and evidence in a text support the author's claims.	• Essays in text set • *Only in America* podcast • *What If You Were an Immigrant?* TED Talk

(Continued)

Table 3.3   Unit Overview and General Teaching Ideas (*Continued*)

Weeks Eight–Nine
- Inquiry Project

Common Core Standards	Some Related Texts
• Range of Reading and Level of Text Complexity: • CCSS.ELA-LITERACY.RH.9-10.10 By the end of grade 10, read and comprehend history/social studies texts in grades 9–10 text complexity band independently and proficiently. • Integration of Knowledge and Ideas: • CCSS.ELA-LITERACY.RH.9-10.7 Integrate quantitative or technical analysis (e.g., charts and research data) with qualitative analysis in print or digital text.	• Students may choose any of the sources in the text set the teacher provides depending on their topic.

- **Immigration Today (15 Minutes)**

Read this article from Newsela: Washington State Officials Are Outraged Over the Policy of Separating Immigrant Families: https://newsela.com/read/lib-washington-immigrants-officials-trump/id/45036/?collection_id=339&search_id=9ca30b66-b231-4744-bc7a-23cb17088561

Provide a description or example of the phrases below using a sentence from the article.

1. Origin
2. Family separation
3. Inhumane
4. Zero-tolerance policy
5. Trauma

- **Extension**

If you have students who finish work ahead of schedule, you can share this other article with them until you wait for the rest of the class to finish and to start the discussion.

Immigrants Put America First: In Coming Here, They Affirm Our Values | Bush Center An Essay by Carlos Gutierrez, Former U.S. Secretary of Commerce: https://www.bushcenter.org/catalyst/democracy/gutierrez-immigrants-validate-values.html

- **Whole-Class Discussion and Exit Ticket (10 Minutes)**

The teacher will lead a whole class discussion reflecting on the definitions, concepts, and guiding questions of the texts studied. Students write their main takeaway from the lesson on a sticky note and post it on the wall as their exit ticket.

Adaptations for Particular Student Populations:

- **For Spanish Speakers**

Spanish speakers can read this article about the Chinese Exclusion Act in Spanish from Newsela:

U.S. History: Inmigración china y las Leyes de Exclusión de los Chinos https://newsela.com/read/lib-latino-us-immigration-economic-factors-sp anish/id/54422/?collection_id=339&search_id=12fe9435-64ec-4359-af78 -d227587cac62

They can also read this other article about Latino immigration to the United States and the factors that push this phenomenon: Inmigración Latina a Estados Unidos: Factores económicos. https://newsela.com/read/lib-latino -us-immigration-economic-factors-spanish/id/54422/?collection_id=339&s earch_id=12fe9435-64ec-4359-af78-d227587cac62

To make the issue more relevant, students can complete an activity in which they compare and contrast how people perceive immigrant in the United Stated with a Latin American country.

- **Instructions:** Responde la siguiente pregunta y prepara una presentación de dos minutos luego de estudiar el tema de la inmigración de un país específico.

¿Cómo afecta la inmigración el estilo de vida tanto del inmigrante como de los ciudadanos de la nación receptora? Compara esta situación entre un país hispano y los Estados Unidos.
   Short video clips of news reports or interviews that can be used for this task:

- España: https://www.youtube.com/watch?v=XCO3p5R3tF4
- Venezuela: https://www.youtube.com/watch?v=bPCamtgVdtg
- México: https://www.youtube.com/watch?v=MmRbIJMU7GM
- Chile: https://www.youtube.com/watch?v=OxKinqkzvtM
    https://www.youtube.com/watch?v=FwPrpvTpJGg
- Europa/Francia: https://www.youtube.com/watch?v=07h64xYf_sw

Sample Lesson Two: Why People Choose to Immigrate

In this lesson, students will gain a better understanding of the circumstances that push people to migrate through the study of art, audiovisual resources, and printed text. To begin, tell students to complete the bell ringer activity having the question projected on the board as they come into your classroom. Next, provide instructions about the gallery walk activity. Tell students that they need to take their journals with them and walk around the classroom. Also, tell them that they do not need to spend too much time trying to understand the pictures. They should just write their first impression of how they believe immigration is represented. It is important to have a timer displayed on the board for time-keeping purposes. When the timer is up, tell students to sit down and start projecting the images on the screen, asking students to provide their interpretations. After that section is over, give instructions for the essay. Explain the problem question and remind students about expectations when writing an argumentative essay. Ask a student to repeat instructions as a way to confirm that they have understood. For the exit ticket, just project the instructions on the board.

Student-Friendly Learning Targets:
- I can interpret and identify a topic from art.
- I can compare different immigration stories and understand the particular circumstances that push people to migrate.

Duration of the Lesson: 90 minutes (two 45-minute class periods)
Materials Needed: Classroom projector, computers, notebook paper or writing journals, and printed pictures in color
Activities:
- **Bell Ringer Activity (5 Minutes)**

Students respond to the following question: Why is talking about immigration important? This quote is also displayed.

"Looking forward, immigrants and their descendants are projected to account for 88% of U.S. population growth through 2065, assuming current immigration trends continue" (Pew Research Center, 2015).

- **Gallery Walk (20 Minutes)**

Like in a museum gallery, students walk around the classroom looking at ten pictures and paintings that represent immigration. They will write a title they create for the visual and their interpretation of each of them. The pictures and paintings are the ones from the multimodal text set, although different ones can be used. Prior to class, the teacher will print images and tape them to the wall. Students will have 10 minutes to walk around and then the teacher will go over the ten pictures on the projector and ask students what title they assigned to them and why.

- **Immigrant Stories and Current Events (60 Minutes)**

Using the texts listed below, students will write an argumentative essay responding to the following question: Why is it important to understand the stories of immigrants to determine the best types of immigration policies for a country?

Videos

- Dinner with Immigrants: https://www.youtube.com/watch?v=yP3jZkSQrvw
- Illustrated Immigration Visual Essay - 360 Video/Virtual Reality: https://www.youtube.com/watch?v=TFXfcg4KJPU
- Being a Refugee Is Not a Choice: https://www.youtube.com/watch?v=JwkVk16xecw
- Refugee Crisis from Syria - Refugees 360 VR Documentary: https://www.youtube.com/watch?v=z9HEGHOk5hM
- Caravan Immigrants in Mexico: https://www.youtube.com/watch?v=BM1FjXAetr0

Articles from Newsela

- We Come in Peace: Migrants Start Asylum Journey at U.S. Border: https://newsela.com/read/migrants-asylum-US-border/id/47551/?collection_id=339&search_id=6f23b34a-ee59-4def-8c23-ff2eba65acbe
- Americans Want to Share their Homes with Central American Asylum Seekers: https://newsela.com/read/americans-open-homes-asylum-seekers/id/43017/?collection_id=339&search_id=39cc7070-ee8d-4903-9e96-2e8287a01e4c

- **Exit Ticket: Just One Word! (5 Minutes)**

Students describe in one word what they think about the immigrant stories that they listened to or read about.

Adaptations for Particular Student Populations:

- **For Spanish Speakers**

Spanish speakers can replace one of the English videos from above for this one:

- From Mexico to the U.S: El Calvario de los Inmigrantes Centroamericanos para Llegar a Estados Unidos: https://www.youtube.com/watch?v=3k1q8QJaci0

Students can complete tasks, such as the gallery walk and the essay activities, in Spanish.

GUIDELINES FOR A STUDENT INDIVIDUAL INQUIRY PROJECT

The title of this inquiry project is "The Journey." For this project, students will have to read or listen to a text that tells the story of an immigrant. They may choose from the texts in the multimodal text set or others you provide. They will need to present the narrative of the story to the rest of the class in a mode of their preference. The goal is to clearly communicate the journey that the immigrant experienced to reach their final destination. Although many of the stories on the text set are fictional, most of them portray a real narrative of the things that immigrants have to go through when they embark on the journey toward a better life.

SUPPORT FOR EMERGENT BILINGUALS

Since the emergent bilingual population is so diverse, all possible adaptations cannot be provided in this chapter. Teachers need to find texts that apply to their particular student characteristics. Some texts included in the multimodal text set can be used, but educators are encouraged to do some research with the help of their school librarian to find texts that are available in their EBs' languages. (See East West Discovery Press for multilingual children's books and Wonderopolis Immersive Reader feature for informational text in various languages.) Focus on student learning by encouraging them to complete tasks in their preferred language.

SUPPORT FOR STUDENTS WITH SPECIAL LEARNING NEEDS

In the multi-day lessons in this chapter, consider reducing the amount of tasks for students to help them focus on just one or two. As they are reading, remember that Newsela articles have read-aloud accessibility and Lexile levels can also be adapted to different levels.

TEACHING A MODIFIED UNIT FOR MIDDLE SCHOOL

As an extension to this unit or to use with younger students, teachers can focus on notorious or famous immigrants. Students will research the accomplishment of certain immigrants and their contributions to the United States. They will then present their findings citing their sources in a mode of their preference (e.g., poster boards and digital presentation). They can use these articles to guide their research:

- 17 Famous Immigrants Who Helped Make America Great: https://www.globalcitizen.org/en/content/bet-you-didnt-know-these-game-changers-were-immigr/
- Over Half of $1 Billion Startups Are Founded By Immigrants: https://www.nbcnews.com/news/latino/over-half-1-billion-startups-are-founded-immigrants-n544446

Additionally, younger students can learn about immigration through class read-alouds of some of the picture books in the text set and respond through artwork or poetry. Figure 3.2 is a 5th grade student's poem about immigration, and Figure 3.3 shows a student's artistic response.

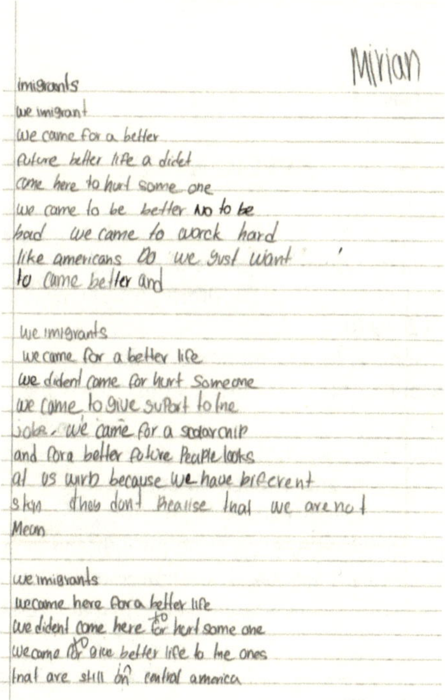
Mirian

imigrants
we imigrant
we came for a better
future better life a didet
come here to hurt some one
we came to be better no to be
bad we came to work hard
like americans do we gust want
to came better and

we imigrants
we came for a better life
we dident come for hurt someone
we came to give suport to the
jobs, we came for a scolarchip
and fora better future People looks
at us wirb because we have diferent
skin they dont realise that we are not
Mean

we imigrants
wecame here for a better life
we dident come here to hert some one
wecame to give better life to the ones
that are still on central america

Figure 3.2 Immigrants. *Mirian Ayala.*

Figure 3.3 Everything Has a Price. *Julio Flores.*

REFERENCES

Budyman, A. (2020, August 20). *Key findings about U.S. immigrants*. Pew Research Center. https://www.pewresearch.org/fact-tank/2020/08/20/key-findings-about-u-s-immigrants/#:~:text=The%20U.S.%20foreign%2Dborn%20population,share%20(4.8%25)%20in%201970.

Merriam-Webster Dictionary. (n.d.). Immigration. In *Merriam-Webster.com dictionary*. Retrieved December 11, 2020, from https://www.merriam-webster.com/dictionary/immigration.

Pew Research Center. (2015). Modern immigration wave brings 59 million to U.S., driving population growth and change through 2065. Retrieved December 11, 2020, from http://www.pewhispanic.org/2015/09/28/modern-immigration-wave-brings-59-million-to-u-s-driving-population-growth-and-change-through-2065/.

Pew Research Center. (2020). Facts on U.S. immigrants, 2018. Retrieved December 11, 2020, from https://www.pewresearch.org/hispanic/2020/08/20/facts-on-u-s-immigrants/.

Portes, A., & Rumbaut, R. G. (2014). *Immigrant America: A portrait* (4th ed.). University of California Press.

Stewart, M. A. (2017). *Understanding adolescent immigrants: Moving toward an extraordinary discourse for extraordinary youth*. Lexington Books.

Part II

THE INFLUENCES OF LATIN AMERICA ON U.S. CULTURE AND SOCIETY

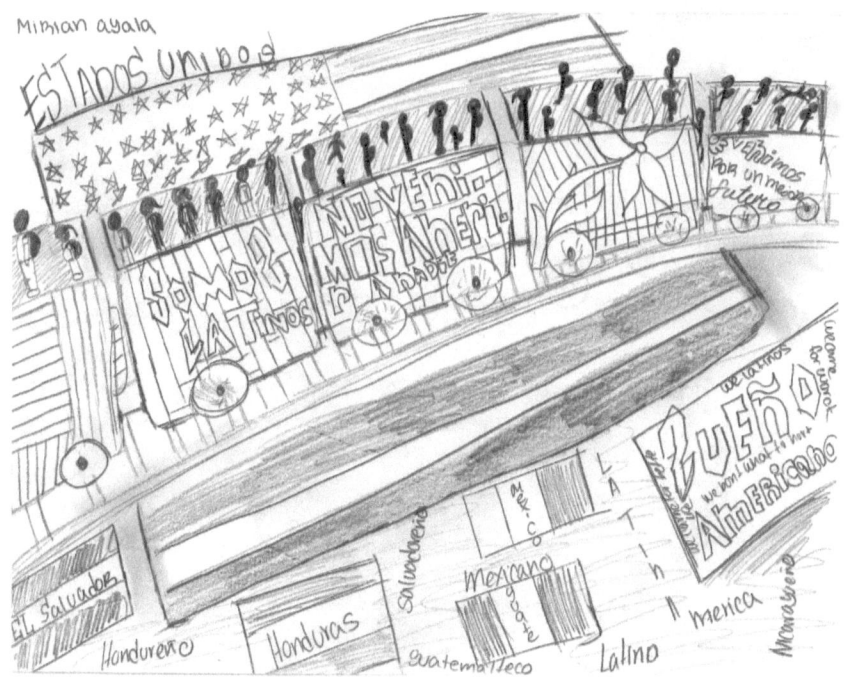

Figure PII.1 Estados Unidos. *Mirian Ayala.*

Leila Cobo (2021) wrote about how Latin music has come to influence not only American music, but also music from throughout the world. These influences are not limited to music. Latinx people influence politics, sports, and the arts. We see more traditional notions of influence, such as César Chávez and Dolores Huerta, advocating for farm workers' rights, to more modern examples such as Alexandria Ocasio-Cortez attracting one of the largest audiences on Twitch while playing the popular video game Among Us and using her audience to raise millions of dollars for victims of Winter Storm Uri in Texas. These influencers are more than just tokens in our American society; they are part of the fabric of what we call America.

The following section brings Latinx people to the forefront and allows students from these backgrounds to see themselves not as subjugated people who are often victims in traditional histories of America, but as the positive change agents in modern America.

Cobo, L. (2021). *Decoding "Despacito": An oral history of Latin music.* Vintage.

Chapter 4

Latinx Influencers

Past and Present Contributions to America's Greatness

Margarita Ramos-Rivera

Figure 4.1 Roberto Clemente. *Angela Gonzalez.*

THEME AND RATIONALE

There is currently a debate about the terms *Hispanic*, *Latino*, and *Latinx* (García, 2020). People who identify with these communities, while sharing similar cultural traditions, also have many differences. Before teachers plan a unit of study, it is important to understand this evolution if they want to best meet students' needs. It is generally accepted that Hispanic refers to people with a Spanish-speaking background. Latino and Latina, on the other hand, refer to those from the geographic region of Latin America. This includes much of Central and South America, as well as the Caribbean. Similarly, these terms have recently been modified using the word Latinx as a gender-neutral alternative to Latino (García, 2020). However, all of these terms have the Spanish language in common. Although they represent people of different cultures and histories, they have changed U.S. history forever.

In the United States, Hispanics are the largest minority. But what have they accomplished and how have they reshaped U.S. history? We can see thousands of Latinx students out there and in our classrooms, but their histories are not always studied in depth in the average U.S. curriculum. Educators have traditionally taught influencers in the Social Studies and Language Arts curricula such as big inventors, scientific innovators, and social reformers like George Washington. Oftentimes, current Latinx influencers are absent. However, when students see themselves in the curriculum, this can fortify their interest in the topic and develop their identity, culture, and self-esteem.

According to Freire (2018), students must construct new knowledge from knowledge they already possess. Teachers must learn how the students understand the world so that the teacher understands how the student can learn. Further, many of our Latinx students will also be bilinguals who are exposed to both Spanish and English, among other languages. Translanguaging classroom practices encourage students to use their whole language repertoire to make meaningful connections from the curriculum to their lives. Translanguaging practices indicate that bilingual students have one unitary linguistic repertoire from which they select features appropriate to communicate according to the external context (García & Li Wei, 2014). Language is part of the culture and part of students' identity. If we deny students the opportunity to use their language, we are denying a part of their identity and, sadly sending a message of non-acceptance.

Consequently, drawing from resources in both Spanish and English, this curriculum unit focuses on detailing the importance of Hispanics, Latinos, or Latinx individuals in the United States. Teaching this unit will allow students to understand and think critically about Latinx individuals' contributions to our society, politics, arts, and entertainment.

UNIT GOALS

This unit will empower educators to use critical thinking to deepen, appreciate, and discover Latinx influencers. Students will build new knowledge about the different ways in which Latinx communities and individuals contribute to the development of the United States through the different perspectives of various people. The Latinx influencers found in this unit of study serve our bilingual students just as they served Sonia Sotomayor, as mirrors. "Books were mirrors of my very own universe" (Sotomayor, 2018, n. p.).

Although geared toward pre-adolescents in the 4th grade, this unit can also be applied to middle and even high school classrooms.

MULTIMODAL TEXT SET

Multimodal text options are included to provide differentiation and choice for adolescent students. The use of videos and songs also provides a unique way to teach about Latinx influences. The texts center on members of the Latinx community in the United States who have stood out in the areas of politics, science, sports, and the arts. These texts focus on three primary influencers from the Latinx community: Sonia Sotomayor, Roberto Clemente, and Lin Manual-Miranda. There are also many texts about other Latinx influencers as well.

Sonia Sotomayor (1954–)

- Kramer, B. (2016). *National Geographic readers: Sonia Sotomayor*. National Geographic Kids.
- Sotomayor, S. (2018). *Turning pages: My life story*. Philomel Books.
- The Daily Show with Trevor Noah. (2019, September 23). *Sonia Sotomayor - "Just Ask!" and life as a Supreme Court Justice - The Daily Show* [Video]. YouTube. https://www.youtube.com/watch?v=Nztz3yuF3lY&list=LLEZvoGChYWcgIlGBAeR83Fg&index=173
- Van Tol, A. (2010). *Sonia Sotomayor: Supreme Court Justice*. Crabtree Publishing.

Roberto Clemente (1934–1972)

- Buckley, J. (2018). *Who was Roberto Clemente?* Findaway World.
- bumfromph (2018, June 5). *Roberto Clemente's final interview, October 1972* [Video]. YouTube. https://www.youtube.com/watch?v=RFEH5nxSoKc
- Franchino, V. (2007). *Life skills biographies: Roberto Clemente*. Cherry Lake Publishing.
- Gigliotti, J. (2013). *I am Roberto Clemente*. Scholastic.
- Gigliotti, J. (2014). *Soy Roberto Clemente* (U. Simon, Illus.). Scholastic.

- MLB. (2021). *2020 Roberto Clemente award.* https://www.mlb.com/community/roberto-clemente-award
- On'ry Waymore. (2016, June 4). *Roberto Clemente tribute-The greatest plays & games in his career ending in tragedy* [Video]. YouTube. https://www.youtube.com/watch?v=8dO1CesFJ-s

Lin-Manuel Miranda (1980–)

- Good Morning America (2020, June 22). *Lin-Manuel Miranda talks about 'Hamilton!' coming soon on Disney+ l GMA* [Video]. YouTube. https://www.youtube.com/watch?v=tD36x-DJXZg
- Kramer, B. (2017). *Lin-Manuel Miranda: Award-winning musical writer.* Abdo Publishing.
- Kraus, S. (2016). *Beyond words: Lin-Manuel Miranda.* Teacher Created Materials.
- Miranda, L.-M. (2020). *Home page.* https://www.linmanuel.com/
- Miranda, L.-M. (2018). *Gmorning, gnight! Little pep talks for me and you.* Random House.
- Scaletta, K. (2021). *Trailblazers: Lin-Manuel Miranda: Raising theater to new heights.* Random House Books for Young Children.
- TODAY. (2018, July 23). *Lin-Manuel Miranda full interview with Savannah Guthrie - TODAY* [Video]. YouTube. https://www.youtube.com/watch?v=zHv4G1xw3As
- Walt Disney Studios (2020, June 21). *Hamilton - Official Trailer - Disney+* [Video]. YouTube. https://www.youtube.com/watch?v=DSCKfXpAGHc

Multimodal Text Set That Connects to the Theme

- Ada, A. F., Campoy, F. I., & Diaz, D. (2013). *¡Sí! Somos Latinos.* Charlesbridge.
- Ada, A. F., Campoy, F. I., & Diaz, D. (2013). *Yes! We are Latinos.* Charlesbridge.
- Auñon-Chancellor, S. (n.d.). Astronaut biography. Ellen Ochoa. https://www.nasa.gov/sites/default/files/atoms/files/aunon.pdf
- Herrera, J. F., & Colón, R. l. (2014). *Portraits of Hispanic American heroes.* Dial Books for Young Readers.
- Latham, D. (2006). *Ellen Ochoa: Reach for the stars!* Bearport Pub.
- Menéndez, J. (2021). *Latinitas: Celebrating big dreamers in history!* Godwin Books.
- Reynoso, N. (2020). *Be bold! Be brave! 11 Latinas who made U.S. history.* Con Todo Press.

- Reynoso, N. (2020). *Fearless trailblazers: 11 Latinos who made U.S. history.* Con Todo Press.
- Van Tol, A. (2010). *Dolores Huerta: Voice for the working poor.* Crabtree Publishing.

SAMPLE LESSONS

Table 4.1 illustrates a general overview of the unit. The sample lessons are designed to integrate both language arts and social studies standards while engaging in reading, writing, viewing, and listening to various texts. In these lessons, 4th grade students will use critical thinking to discover Latinx influencers in the United States and make connections to the texts about their lives and legacies.

Sample Lesson One: Discovering Current Latinx Influencers

This lesson will introduce students to current Latinx influencer Sonia Sotomayor. Students will discuss and create a product over what they learned from Sonia Sotomayor's contribution to the United States and explain their connections.

Content Objective: I can make different types of connections.
Language Objective: I can discuss with my partner what the book reminded me of.
Key Vocabulary:
- Text
- Metacognition
- Connections—the teacher creates vocabulary cards with a visual, definition, sentence, and synonym of each term such as the one below in Figure 4.2.

Warm-up: Divide students into groups and have them discuss the meaning of the words *text*, *metacognition*, and *connections* located on the vocabulary cards with a visual, definition, word used in a sentence, and synonym for each term. Then, show the students the PowToon video on YouTube, What Are Text Connections?, to further explain how they will make connections to the texts. The video may be found at the following website: https://www.youtube.com/watch?v=gP59YwkBuWs

Presentation/Modeling/Mini-Lesson: The focus is on making different types of connections using multimedia texts. Explain to students that you are going to practice the comprehension strategy of making connections to

Table 4.1 Unit Overview and General Teacher Ideas

Week One
- Reading mentor texts, biographies, and informational text about Latinx influencers
- Influence of Supreme Court Justice Sonia Sotomayor

Common Core Standards	Some Related Texts
• CCSS.ELA-LITERACY.RL.4.7 Make connections between the text of a story or drama and a visual or oral presentation of the text, identifying where each version reflects specific descriptions and directions in the text. • CCSS.ELA-LITERACY.L.4.4 Determine or clarify the meaning of unknown and multiple-meaning words and phrases based on grade 4 reading and content, choosing flexibly from a range of strategies. • CCSS.ELA-LITERACY.W.4.2 Write informative/explanatory texts to examine a topic and convey ideas and information Range of Reading and Level of Text Complexity.	• Sotomayor, S. (2018). *Turning pages: My life story* (L. Delacre, Illus.). Philomel Books. • Kramer, B. (2016). *National Geographic readers: Sonia Sotomayor*. National Geographic Kids. • Van Tol, A. (2010). *Sonia Sotomayor: Supreme Court Justice*. Crabtree Publishing.

Week Two
- Conveying opinions
- Synthesizing Information
- Influence of Lin-Manuel-Miranda and Roberto Clemente

Common Core Standards	Some Related Texts
• CCSS.ELA-LITERACY.RL.4.9 Compare and contrast the treatment of similar themes and topics (e.g., the opposition of good and evil) and patterns of events (e.g., the quest) in stories, myths, and traditional literature from different cultures. • CCSS.ELA-LITERACY.RL.4.7 Make connections between the text of a story or drama and a visual or oral presentation of the text, identifying where each version reflects specific descriptions and directions in the text.	• Mentor Text- *EPIC- Clemente's Biography Electronic Book* by Vicky Franchino. https://www.getepic.com/app/read/10606 • Buckley, J. (2018). *Who was Roberto Clemente?* Findaway World. • Kramer, B. (2017). *Lin-Manuel Miranda: Award-winning musical writer*. Abdo Publishing. • Kraus, S. (2016). *Beyond words: Lin-Manuel Miranda*. Teacher Created Materials.

Weeks Three–Four
- Expressing knowledge through multimodal projects

(Continued)

Table 4.1 Unit Overview and General Teacher Ideas (*Continued*)

Common Core Standards	Some Related Texts
• CCSS.ELA-LITERACY.RI.4.10 By the end of the year, read and comprehend informational texts, including history/social studies, science, and technical texts, in grade 4 text complexity band proficiently, with scaffolding as needed at the high end of the range. • CCSS.ELA-LITERACY.W.4.7 Conduct short research projects that build knowledge through investigation of different aspects of a topic.	• Herrera, J. F., & Colón, R. I. (2014). *Portraits of Hispanic American heroes.* Dial Books for Young Readers. • Reynoso, N. (2020). *Fearless trailblazers: 11 Latinos who made U.S. history.* Con Todo Press. • Reynoso, N. (2020). *Be bold! be brave! 11 Latinas who made U.S. history.* Con Todo Press.

find ways that students can personally relate to a text. Discuss the following kinds of connections:
- Text-to-self
- Text-to-text
- Text-to-world

Then, explain your different connections to a book you have recently read with the class. Explain how your connections fit into each of these three categories. You may create an anchor chart with the three kinds of connections to help students understand.

Guided Practice/Active Engagement: Show students the book cover of the mentor text: *Turning Pages* by Sonia Sotomayor. Allow students to turn and talk about what they think the story's point of view is and if they have an initial connection with the story.

Read aloud this book about Sonia Sotomayor and stop at various points to discuss how she became the first Latina Supreme Court Justice with students. In the end, ask students the following questions: Did you like the story? Why or why not? Where will your journey lead you? Allow students to turn and talk to peers. Then, discuss your own text-to-self, text-to-text, and text-to-world connections with the book. Ask students to write their own connections as guided by these questions: What does this story remind you of? Can you relate to the characters in the story? Does anything in this story remind you of anything in your own life, with another text, or the world?

Independent Practice: Then, provide students with copies of books from the text set about Sotomayor and have them write their new connections.

Assessment: Observe if students are able to explain connections. Put them in small groups and have them discuss their connections with their group as you observe their ability to do so. Table 4.2 is a rubric you can use to assess each student's progress.

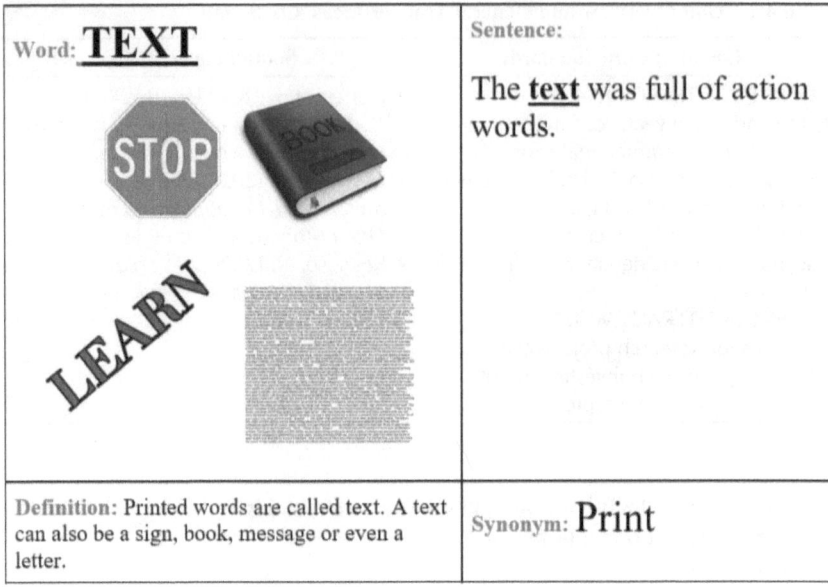

Figure 4.2 Vocabulary Card Example.

Closure: As a whole class, allow students to share their connections to texts they read or viewed. Discuss evidence in the text that prompted those connections. Students can explain how connections help them have a deeper understanding.

Extension: Connection Web Activity: Students use a graphic organizer to expand on connections they have made to a text and use those details to write an essay about their response to the book.

Table 4.2 Assessment Rubric for Making Connections to Text

	Level 1 Beginning	Level 2 Developing	Level 3 Meets Standard
Making Connections	The student could neither explain connections or talk about what the text reminds him/her, nor could he/she explain with evidence. Teacher prompting was needed.	The student is able to explain connections and discuss what part of the text prompted those connections. The student cannot explain how the connections helped with comprehension of the text. Teacher prompting was necessary.	The student is able to explain connections and discuss evidence in the text that prompted those connections. The student can explain how connections help him/her have a deeper understanding. No teacher prompting was needed.

Sample Lesson 2: Writing a Book Review

This lesson will occur after students have already learned about Sotomayor, Clemente, and Miranda, as well as other Latinx influencers in the unit. Students will discuss and create a product over what they learned.

Content Objective: I can express my opinion by creating a book review of my favorite Latinx influencer.

Language Objective: I can describe the contributions of my favorite Latinx influencer and justify my response with my partner.

Key Vocabulary:
- Opinion
- Facts
- Justify

Create vocabulary cards for each vocabulary word like the example in the first sample lesson.

Warm-Up: Divide students into partners and allow them to review the vocabulary cards and discuss the key terms.

Presentation/Modeling/Mini-Lesson: Explain to students that they will evaluate a nonfiction book by writing their opinions through a book review. Read *Portraits of Hispanic American heroes* or another text to the students. As you read, stop and provide your evaluation of the text based on facts to justify your opinion.

Guided Practice/Active Engagement: Then, explain a book review template you create for your students. Examples of the template I created are shown in Figures 4.3 and 4.4. You can create this template by using the following questions:
- What is the book about?
- What is your opinion of the book?
- What facts did you find the most interesting in the book?
- Do you think other people would like to read this book?
- How many stars would you give this book out of five? Why? Justify your opinion.

Explain what you might write for the book you read together in the previous part of the lesson. Allow students to discuss the book they would like to choose and what they might write about, using the guiding questions, with a partner.

Independent Practice: Allow students to locate the book (or multimedia text) they would like to review. Students should look for text evidence that supports their opinion. They will use the book review template you have created with the guiding questions to complete their review.

Figure 4.3 Student Work Sample about Lin-Manuel Miranda. *Alejandra Vanegas.*

Assessment: Listen to students' discussions to observe if they are able to explain and justify their opinions to their partners. Observe students' ability to complete the book review template.

Closure: Allow students to share their book reviews. Display students' work on the walls for the whole school to value their hard work and mastery.

Extension: Students can compose a multimodal display of one of the Latinx influencers they learned about as shown in Figures 4.3 and 4.4.

SUPPORT FOR EMERGENT BILINGUALS

Emergent bilingual students will have varying English and home language proficiency levels. Provide books and other written or multimodal materials in alternate formats such as audio, digital text, and modified versions.

Figure 4.4 Student Work Sample about Ellen Ochoa. *Kelsy Gomez.*

Teachers can also help students add their language to the vocabulary cards, making bilingual versions.

SUPPORT FOR STUDENTS WITH SPECIAL LEARNING NEEDS

Connected learners (those who are learning remotely) and other students with special needs could work with the digital template of the texts when reading online. You can also work with your school's librarian to locate texts with varying Lexile levels for your students. Lastly, instead of writing a book review, students can record their book review orally.

TEACHING A MODIFIED UNIT FOR HIGH SCHOOL

High school students can deeply explore what an influencer entails in today's world and how someone becomes an influencer. Students can study different

Latinx influencers from various fields to explore who they think has the most influence, with whom, and why. They can engage with more mature texts such as these biographies and autobiographies of Latinx influencers.

- Manzano, S. (2015). *Becoming Maria: Love and chaos in the South Bronx.* Scholastic Press.
- Ortiz, D., & Massarotti, T. (2007). *Big Papi: My story of big dreams and big hits.* St. Martin's Press.
- Sotomayor, S. (2013). *My beloved world.* Knopf.

REFERENCES

Freire, P. (2018). *Pedagogy of the oppressed.* Bloomsbury Academic.

García, I. (2020). Cultural insights for planners: Understanding the terms Hispanic, Latino, and Latinx. *Journal of the American Planning Association, 86*(4), 393–402. https://doi.org/10.1080/01944363.2020.1758191

García, O., & Wei, L. (2014). *Translanguaging: Language, bilingualism, and education.* Palgrave Macmillan.

Sotomayor, S. (2018). *Turning pages: My life story.* Philomel Books.

Vygotsky, L. (1935/2011). The dynamics of the schoolchild's mental development in relation to teaching and learning. *Journal of Cognitive Education and Psychology, 10*(2), 198–211. https://doi.org/10.1891/1945-8959.10.2.198

Chapter 5

Latinas as Change Agents
Feminist Activism in the United States
Juan Borda

Figure 5.1 **Words Matter**. *Severyn McCauley.*

THEME AND RATIONALE

Students attending U.S. public schools pledge allegiance to our nation's flag, a nation of immigrants, which stands for liberty and justice for all. However, these principles of liberty and justice for all have applied mostly to ruling and privileged groups in the past centuries. Within the United States, there have been many contradictory policies, such as segregation and discrimination. Those with power maintain their dominance by reproducing dominant ideologies (Bourdieu, 1977). Albright and Luke (2012) explain that class reproduction is propelled through the socialization of schooling, which often subjugates students' and teachers' human agency and potential.

Marginalized groups have confronted injustices through centuries. There is a need to change unfair social and educational practices by adopting new forms of literacy instruction. According to Freire and Macedo (1987), emancipatory literacy includes two dimensions. The first calls for students to become aware of their histories, experiences, and cultural heritage. The second indicates the need for students to understand the codes and cultures of dominant contexts. This unit on Latina activists includes notable people from the Hispanic community. The women included have shown exemplary character and leadership characteristics that make them unique. They have advocated for social justice, challenging dominant ideologies. A major objective is to expose students to read and inquire using critical lenses. Reading always involves critical understandings and inferences to reconceptualize the meaning of the text (Freire & Macedo, 1987). A critical approach to the unit helps students to build their self-identity and understand their context and world.

UNIT GOALS

This unit will allow students to research some of the most prominent Latina activists who have demonstrated courage, integrity, and leadership abilities to advocate for social justice and denounce inequity. Although these individuals have lived in different eras, ranging from 1890 to the present, they share the same ideals of fairness and justice. By selecting people from different periods, the students can better understand the historical context and its significance. Students are encouraged to situate the activists in their specific period and critically analyze the issues and factors affecting their decisions.

Finally, building students' identities is a significant objective of the unit. Each student brings their prior experiences with them as they make meaning with the new content. Students can make personal connections with the

Latina activists to expand their understanding and to become critical thinkers. Throughout this unit, cooperative learning and class discussion are encouraged to understand the content deeply.

MULTIMODAL TEXT SET

Multimodal digital texts are included for each of the four activists in this unit: Jovita Idár, Dolores Huerta, Sonia Sotomayor, and Alexandria Ocasio-Cortez. Texts in various languages, reading levels, and modes (e.g. audio, image, text) are included so students have equitable access to information. These texts were purposefully selected to focus on building students' vocabulary in two main categories: activism and character traits.

Activism Vocabulary: civil rights, bilingualism, democratic institutions, equity, identity, inclusion, poverty, racism, sexism, segregation

Character Trait Vocabulary: honest, leader, brave, thoughtful, happy, inventive, creative, independent, intelligent, imaginative, successful, responsible, courageous, unselfish, respectful, considerate, helpful

Multimodal texts related to each of the four activists follow:

Jovita Idár (1885–1946)

- Alexander, K. L. (n.d.) Jovita Idár. National Women's History Museum. https://www.womenshistory.org/education-resources/biographies/jovita-idar
- BESE. Hidden Figures: Jovita Idár. https://www.youtube.com/watch?v=PYJWF11N4l0
- Jovita Idár. Digital Repository Humanities Texas. https://www.humanities-texas.org/archives/digital-repository/jovita-idar
- Footprints. Jovita Idár | Mexican American journalist Civil rights worker. https://www.youtube.com/watch?v=UosY4pf9a5M
- Gibson, K. G. (2012). *Jovita Idár* (Latinos in American History). Mitchell Lane.
- Medina, J. (2020). Overlooked no more: Jovita Idár, who promoted rights of Mexican-Americans and women. *New York Times.* https://www.nytimes.com/2020/08/07/obituaries/jovita-idar-overlooked.html

Dolores Huerta (1930–)

- Biography.com Editors. Dolores Huerta Biography. https://www.biography.com

- Brown, M., Cepeda, J., & Valencia, C. (2010). *Side by side: The story of Dolores Huerta and Cesar Chavez = Lado a lado: La historia de Dolores Huerta y César Chávez* (1st ed.). Rayo.
- C-SPAN. Dolores Huerta on the C-SPAN Networks. https://www.c-span.org/person/?3128/DoloresHuerta
- Dolores Huerta Foundation for Community Organizing. https://doloreshuerta.org/
- Good Morning America (2020). Dolores Huerta is the fearless labor activist who coined the positive protest slogan "si se puede." https://www.youtube.com/watch?v=I3ZyUDAh4B0
- One Life: Dolores—Google Arts and Culture—Slideshow of Images
- Santana, C., & Benso, B. (2018). *Dolores. Rebel. Activist. Feminist. Mother.* PBS.
- *New York Times*. Various articles in the *New York Times*. https://www.nytimes.com/
- Warren, S. (2012). *Dolores Huerta: A hero to migrant workers*. Marshall Cavendish Children's.

Sonia Sotomayor (1954–)

- Bernier-Grand, C. T., & Gonzalez, T. (2010). *Sonia Sotomayor: Supreme court justice=Jueza de la corte Suprema*. Marshall Cavendish Childrens.
- Biography.com Editors. *Sonia Sotomayor Biography*. https://www.biography.com/law-figure/sonia-sotomayor
- C-SPAN. Conversation with Supreme Court Justice Sotomayor. https://www.c-span.org/video/?407945-1/conversation-justice-sotomayor
- Krull, K. (2015). *Women who broke the rules: Sonia Sotomayor*. Bloomsbury USA Childrens.
- Sotomayor, S. (2013). *Mi mundo adorado*. Vintage Español.
- Sotomayor, S. (2013). *My beloved world*. Knopf.
- Sotomayor, S., & Delacre, L. (2018). *Turning pages: My life story*. Philomel Books.
- Sotomayor, S., Delacre, L., & Mlawer, T. (2018). *Pasando páginas: La historia de mi vida*. Philomel Books.
- Sotomayor, S., & López, R. (2019). *Just ask! Be different, be brave, be you*. Philomel Books.
- Sotomayor, S., Lopez, R., & Mlawer, T. (2019). *¡Solo pregunta! Sé diferente, sé valiente, sé tú*. Philomel Books.
- Stine, M. (2017). *Who is Sonia Sotomayor?* Penguin Workshop.
- The Daily Show with Trevor Noah. Sonia Sotomayor—"Just Ask!" & Life as a Supreme Court Justice. https://www.youtube.com/watch?v=Nztz3yuF3lY

- Winter, J., Rodriguez, E., & Palacios, A. (2009). *Sonia Sotomayor: A judge grows in the Bronx = La juez que creció en el Bronx* (1st ed.). Atheneum Books for Young Readers.

Alexandria Ocasio-Cortez (1989–)

- Anderson, K., & Gutierrez, M. (2021). *Who is Alexandria Ocasio-Cortez?* Penguin Workshop.
- Biography.com Editors. Alexandria Ocasio-Cortez Biography. https://www.biography.com/political-figure/alexandria-ocasio-cortez
- Jones, B. & Trotman, K. (2020). *Queens of the resistance: Alexandria Ocasio-Cortez: A biography*. Plume.
- Lears, R. (Director). (2019). *Knock down the house*. Netflix documentary.
- Maxouris, C. & Ahmed, S. (2017). Alexandria Ocasio-Cortez's campaign shoes to join museum exhibition. CNN. https://www.cnn.com/style/article/alexandria-ocasio-cortez-shoes-style-trnd/index.html
- Newsela (2018). Young Politicians Use Social Media to Share What Their Jobs Are Really Like. https://newsela.com/read/Alexandria-Ocasio-Cortez-instagram/id/47767/
- The Daily Show with Trevor Noah. Alexandria Ocasio-Cortez—Bringing Moral Courage to American Politics. The Daily Show. https://www.youtube.com/watch?v=dUmIdCClbTE

SAMPLE LESSONS

Table 5.1 contains a unit overview with general teaching goals. The sample lessons include the *TRANSLATE* (Teaching Reading and New Strategic Language Approaches to English learners) strategy. This strategy incorporates students' heritage language practices and recognizes culturally relevant pedagogy and bilingualism (Puzio et al., 2017). The *TRANSLATE* instructional strategy supports a translanguaging pedagogy, acknowledging that bilingual students have one unitary linguistic repertoire from which they select features appropriate to the context (García & Li Wei, 2014). The sample lessons are designed to last for several class periods. Each teacher can adapt the lessons to the needs of their classroom and schedule.

Sample Lesson One: Jovita Idár

Content Objective: Students will identify and analyze how Jovita Idár's background influenced her identity and personality. Students will identify

Table 5.1 Unit Overview and Teaching Goals

Week One
- Introduction to activism
- Building identity through Latina activist inquiry
- Jovita Idár

Common Core Standards	Some Related Texts
• CCSS.ELA-LITERACY.RL.11-12.1 Cite strong and thorough textual evidence to support the analysis of what the text says explicitly as well as inferences drawn from the text, including determining where the text leaves matters uncertain. • CCSS.ELA-LITERACY.W.11-12.9 Draw evidence from literary or informational texts to support analysis, reflection, and research. • CCSS.ELA-LITERACY.W.11-12.1 Write arguments to support claims in an analysis of substantive topics or texts, using valid reasoning and relevant and sufficient evidence.	• Medina, J. (2020). Overlooked no more: Jovita Idár, who promoted the rights of Mexican Americans and women. *New York Times*. https://www.nytimes.com/2020/08/07/obituaries/jovita-idar-overlooked.html. • Alexander, K. L. (n.d.). Jovita Idár. National Women's History Museum. https://www.womenshistory.org/education-resources/biographies/jovita-idar

Week Two
- Dolores Huerta
- Civil Rights

Common Core Standards	Some Related Texts
• CCSS.ELA-LITERACY.RI.11-12.2 Determine two or more central ideas of a text and analyze their development over the course of the text, including how they interact and build on one another to provide a complex analysis; provide an objective summary of the text. • CCSS.ELA-LITERACY.RI.11-12.7 Integrate and evaluate multiple sources of information presented in different media or formats (e.g., visually, quantitatively) as well as in words in order to address a question or solve a problem.	• Santana, C. & Benso, B. (2018). Dolores. Rebel. Activist. Feminist. Mother. PBS.—Documentary • Dolores Huerta on the C-SPAN Networks. https://www.c-span.org/person/?3128/DoloresHuerta

Table 5.1 Unit Overview and Teaching Goals (*Continued*)

- CCSS.ELA-LITERACY.W.11-12.2
Write informative/explanatory texts to examine and convey complex ideas, concepts, and information clearly and accurately through the effective selection, organization, and analysis of content.

Week Three
- Sonia Sotomayor
- Judicial branch of government

Common Core Standards	Some Related Texts
CCSS.ELA-LITERACY.RI.11-12.7 Integrate and evaluate multiple sources of information presented in different media or formats (e.g., visually, quantitatively) as well as in words in order to address a question or solve a problem. CCSS.ELA-LITERACY.W.11-12.2 Write informative/explanatory texts to examine and convey complex ideas, concepts, and information clearly and accurately through the effective selection, organization, and analysis of content.	• Sonia Sotomayor—CNN.com—Biography • Bernier-Grand, C. T., & Gonzalez, T. (2010). Sonia Sotomayor: Supreme court justice=Jueza de la corte Suprema. Marshall Cavendish Childrens.—Illustrated Poetry • Winter, J., Rodríguez, E., & Palacios, A. (2009). Sonia Sotomayor: A judge grows in the Bronx = La juez que creció en el Bronx (1st ed.). Atheneum Books for Young Readers.—Picture Book

Week Four
- Alexandria Ocasio-Cortez
- Legislative branch of government

Common Core Standards	Some Related Texts
CCSS.ELA-LITERACY.RI.11-12.7 Integrate and evaluate multiple sources of information presented in different media or formats (e.g., visually, quantitatively) as well as in words in order to address a question or solve a problem. CCSS.ELA-LITERACY.W.11-12.2 Write informative/explanatory texts to examine and convey complex ideas, concepts, and information clearly and accurately through the effective selection, organization, and analysis of content.	• Alexandria Ocasio-Cortez—Bringing Moral Courage to American Politics. The Daily Show. https://www.youtube.com/watch?v=dUmldCClbTE • Newsela (2018). *Young Politicians Use Social Media To Share What Their Jobs Are Really Like.* https://newsela.com/read/Alexandria-Ocasio-Cortez-instagram/id/47767/

(*Continued*)

Table 5.1 Unit Overview and Teaching Goals (*Continued*)

Weeks Five–Six • Inquiry Project	
Common Core Standards	**Some Related Texts**
• CCSS.ELA-LITERACY.RI.11-12.7 Integrate and evaluate multiple sources of information presented in different media or formats (e.g., visually, quantitatively) as well as in words in order to address a question or solve a problem. • CCSS.ELA-LITERACY.W.11-12.2 Write informative/explanatory texts to examine and convey complex ideas, concepts, and information clearly and accurately through the effective selection, organization, and analysis of content.	• Biography.com • Britannica

and discuss how Jovita Idár's leadership contributed to promoting changes in her community.

Language Objective: Students will write a report and give a presentation about Jovita Idár. Students will work individually and collaboratively to research and present to the class.

Key Vocabulary: activist, racism, Texas Rangers, Mexican Americans, sexism, injustice, Jim Crow laws, First Amendment, segregation, social justice

Procedures:
1. **Introduction:** Read the lesson objectives.
2. **Activate Prior Knowledge:** The teacher will ask students to brainstorm prior knowledge about facts in the 1900s, and to list words to define identity and justice. They can work collaboratively in groups of three. Students will write their ideas on a page. Then ask students to briefly discuss their prior knowledge responses.
3. **Motivation:** Play the video *Footprints*. Then, the teacher leads a wholeclass discussion to make connections between current events at the local, state, and national levels and the video. Use the following questions:
   - Can you make connections regarding freedom of speech at that time and freedom of speech currently?
   - Can you identify similarities and differences between the people in the beginning of the 1900s and people in the present time?
   - Why do those similarities or differences continue or change?

Students are prompted to first reflect in their journals then discuss with their partner or small group. Once all students have had the opportunity to both write and speak, the teacher asks for sharing in the whole group.

4. **Learning Activity:** After the discussion, the students are prompted to research the life and contributions of Jovita Idár, paying special attention to the historical time period. Through using the resources in the multimodal text set, they must identify the following items using at least two genres of text.
   - Characteristics of the time period
   - Early life
   - Family
   - Education
   - Obstacles she overcame
   - Major contributions
   - Notable personality traits
   - Legacy
   - How does she inspire you?
   - What do you think her opinion would be on specific modern-day issues?

Table 5.2 Rubric to Guide Inquiry and Assessment

Criteria	Yes	No	?
I found key concepts and identity characteristics about Jovita Idár.			
I made connections between the topic and current situations.			
I generated questions about the topic.			
I used my understanding to make informed conclusions.			

Students use text and images to record their findings on posters in the style of the biographies in *Artists, Writers, Thinkers, Dreamers: Portraits of Fifty Famous Folks & All Their Weird Stuff* (Hancock, 2014). Images from a few of the biographies in this book are found online. Students will use limited text to create a visual biography of Jovita Idár using the information they find. They may complete this with markers, poster boards, and even images they cut from magazines. They may also make a digital version using PicCollage. Then, students display their posters throughout the room, creating a gallery walk for other students to provide feedback. Students can use sticky notes to provide feedback to their peers. If students need support to provide feedback, they can use the following prompts:

- One idea I agree with is _____ because _____.
- One question I have is _____.
- One personal connection I found was_____.

5. **Evaluation:** To end this part of the unit, students create a digital presentation to present their learning of this activist. Students' digital presentations should include key concepts, personal connections, and further research about the activist. Use the rubric in Table 5.2 to help students evaluate their own work.
6. **Extension Activity:** *TRANSLATE*

The following activity is recommended to use with emergent bilingual students, heritage speakers, and even students who might identify as monolingual, but are in a world language class in their school. This strategy follows the *TRANSLATE* instructional strategy (Puzio et al., 2017). The teacher needs to choose an appropriate text for students to translate from English to Spanish or another language. The text can also be in Spanish, and the students work collaboratively to translate it into English. The text should be short yet somewhat challenging such as the example below which is an excerpt of a Newsela article. This activity connects students to text and allows them to think critically about words, phrases, and meaning. After providing students the text, they work together in partners or small groups to determine how to best translate the passage of text. They may use translation apps; however, they need to understand there are many ways to translate some words and phrases and they must understand the audience and context to choose the best translation.

> Idár blocked the door. She told the Texas Rangers to leave. She did this even though she knew the Texas Rangers could be violent. They attacked and even killed Mexicans in Texas. Eventually, the Texas Rangers left. However, they came back the next day. They destroyed the printing presses. Idár was not afraid to take a stand for her beliefs. She believed the press had the right to hold powerful people accountable. She spent her career fighting injustice.

Sample Lesson 2: Alexandria Ocasio-Cortez

Content Objective: Students will synthesize multimodal texts to show how Alexandria Ocasio Cortez's identity and perseverance contribute to building our national identity by promoting change in the community.

Language Objective: Students will read and summarize Alexandria Ocasio Cortez's major achievements and contributions to the community.

Key Vocabulary: honest, leader, brave, thoughtful, happy, inventive, creative, independent, intelligent, imaginative, successful, responsible, courageous, unselfish, respectful, considerate, helpful, determination, activism, sexism, injustice

Procedure:
1. **Introduction:** Read the lesson objectives.
2. **Activate Prior Knowledge:** Students will brainstorm prior knowledge about modern-day activists. They might include Alexandra Ocasio-Cortez. They can work collaboratively in groups of three. Students will record their findings and ideas electronically on a Google Jamboard.
3. **Motivation:** Play the video located on the CNN article website (https://www.cnn.com/style/article/alexandria-ocasio-cortez-shoes-style-trnd/index.html). Lead the class discussion to make connections between current events and the video.
4. **Learning Activity:** Ask students to explain the following words from Ocasio-Cortez in their own words "I was born in a place where your zip code determines your destiny."

    After students write their ideas in their journals, they share with a partner. Then, the teacher shows students an example of a Name Poem that they have created about themselves. After showing the Name Poem template found at ReadWriteThink.org (http://www.readwritethink.org/files/resources/lesson_images/lesson391/NamePoem.pdf), students use

the resources in the text set to write a Name Poem for Alexandria Ocasio-Cortez.
5. **Evaluation:** Students present the final product of their Name Poems.
6. **Extension Activity:** *TRANSLATE*

The teacher provides students with an excerpt from a text such as this paragraph is from a Newsela article (https://newsela.com/read/Alexandria-Ocasio-Cortez-instagram/id/47767/). First, allow students the opportunity to translate individually. Then, put them in groups to translate orally and in writing. Students should be engaged in dialogue about the translation.

> Alexandria Ocasio-Cortez is a Democrat from New York. She was elected to Congress in November. She will serve in the House of Representatives. At 29, she is the youngest woman ever elected to Congress. Like many young adults, Ocasio-Cortez uses Instagram. She likes to share photos and videos. She doesn't always talk politics, though. Sometimes she shares things totally unrelated to her new job. For example, she asked her followers about her leftovers. They told her macaroni that sat in her fridge for a week was probably too old to eat.

GUIDELINES FOR A STUDENT INDIVIDUAL INQUIRY PROJECT

The purpose of the inquiry project is for students to have the choice to select any Latina activist to further research. This can be one of the women already studied, another famous Latina activist, or someone they know in their community. They might find inspiration from this book list on Latinas *Who Made A Difference* by Colorín Colorado: https://www.colorincolorado.org/booklist/latinas-who-made-difference. Students also can view the visually evocative slide shows in GoogleArts&Culture on Ten Inspiring Latins Who've Made History: https://artsandculture.google.com/story/10-inspiring-latinas-who%E2%80%99ve-made-history/NQLCw0ak0_NsKg. Once they have made a selection, they choose three to five items from the following criteria to research the Latina activist:

- Picture book
- Poetry
- Chapter book/novel/biography
- Informational article
- Video/documentary
- Podcast
- Interview (This might be an interview with the activist or an interview with someone who has been inspired by the activist. For example, they could

watch a recorded interview with Dolores Huerta or interview someone in their community who is inspired by Huerta.)

Students collect their data in a research journal using a template such as the Research Paper Scaffold found on ReadWriteThink.org: https://www.readwritethink.org/sites/default/files/resources/lesson_images/lesson1155/scaffold.pdf. Using Writer's Workshop in the classroom, students write a draft, confer with the teacher, and revise their research paper. Then, each student creates a visual representation of their research using Pic Collage, another app that allows them to create both images and text, or a poster board.

SUPPORT FOR EMERGENT BILINGUALS

Make sure you know the languages your EBs, as well as other multilingual students, speak. Do not rely on only the Home Language Survey, but give your students a more in-depth language survey to understand all of the languages in their lives. You may create your own language surveys of use the one available in Spanish and English on this website: https://us.corwin.com/en-us/nam/but-does-this-work-with-english-learners/book273595#free-resources. You can also find it in *But Does This Work with English Learners?* (Stewart & Genova, 2020). Once you have a good understanding of all of your students' languages and their proficiencies with those languages, you can better prepare the *TRANSLATE* extension activities. In addition to text excerpts students collaboratively translate from English to another language, you can use Newsela to find articles in Spanish and Wonderopolis for articles in many different languages when you use the immersive reader feature. Although there are no articles specifically on the four activists in this unit, you will find relevant texts about suffrage (Jovita Idár), civil rights (Dolores Huerta), the Supreme Court (Sonia Sotomayor), and elections in the United States (Alexandra Ocasio-Cortez).

SUPPORT FOR STUDENTS WITH SPECIAL LEARNING NEEDS

For students with special learning needs, provide modified guidelines for individual work such as different sources for research. Some students might work best with a graphic organizer to complete as they read to write down relevant information. Many of the texts have audio options, so allow students to listen to texts in addition to reading. Finally, when students and groups are working on projects, give students a space with limited distractions where they can focus on the learning activities.

TEACHING A MODIFIED UNIT FOR ELEMENTARY OR MIDDLE SCHOOL

Although this unit is designed for an 11th or 12th grade high school class, there are many ways teachers can use the same teaching ideas for upper elementary and middle schools. The text set contains both novels and picture books. For younger grades, teachers might use more of the picture books and the chapter books written for adolescents such as the ones for the *Who Is?* series. Instead of writing a full research paper for their inquiry project, students can take notes about their selected activist to create a visual that includes text and drawing. Figure 5.2 illustrates one student's multimodal creation from their research on Alexandria Ocasio-Cortez.

Figure 5.2 Alexandria Ocasio-Cortez. *Paisley Kleppe.*

REFERENCES

Albright, J., & Luke, A. (2012). *Pierre Bourdieu and literacy education.* Routledge.
Alvermann, D. E. (2017). *Adolescent literacies: A handbook of practice-based research.* Guilford Publications.
Bourdieu, P. (1977). *Outline of a theory of practice.* Cambridge University Press.
Echevarría, J., Vogt, M., & Short, D. J. (2008). *Making content comprehensible for English learners: The SIOP Model.* Pearson.
Freire, P., & Macedo, D. P. (1987). *Literacy: Reading the word the world.* Routledge & Kegan Paul.
García, O., & Wei, L. (2014). *Translanguaging: Language, bilingualism, and education.* Palgrave Macmillan.
Puzio, K., Keys, C., & Jimenez, R. T. (2017). Let's translate! In K. A. Hinchman & D. A. Appleman. (Eds.), *Adolescent literacies: A handbook of practice-based research* (pp. 276–291). Guilford Press.
Stewart, M. A., & Genova, H. (2020). *But does this work with English learners? A guide for English language arts teachers, grades 6–12.* Corwin Press.

Part III

AMERICA'S ORIGINAL SIN

UNDERSTANDING AND RESPONDING TO RACISM

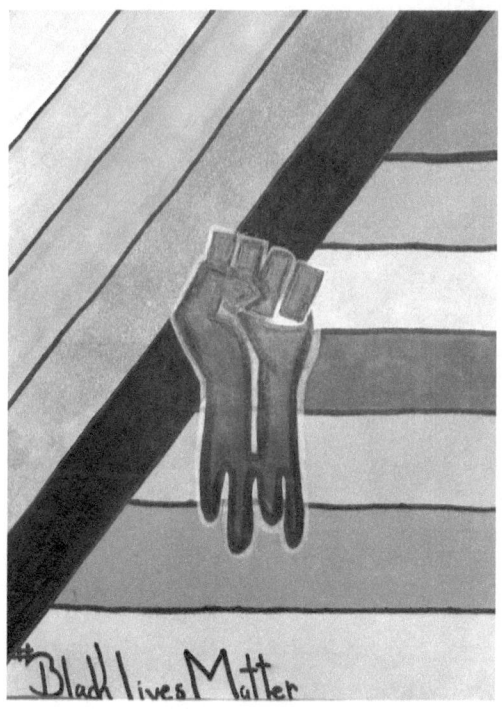

Figure PIII.1 Black Lives Matter. *Estephania Frias.*

The Tulsa Opera recently commissioned a piece from Black composer Daniel Roumain to commemorate the Tulsa race massacres of 1921. They fired him over what they called creative differences, yet what were those differences?

Roumain wanted to end the piece charged with how he felt about America with the lyrics, "God bless America. God damn America." The opera tried to have him change it to repeating "God bless America" or even saying "God help America." This systematic extinguishing of Black voices and Black lives such as George Floyd, Botham Jean, or Breonna Taylor (say their names!) has been happening since Europeans colonized this land.

The following section calls students to critically question America's racist history, examine the systemic racism in the practice of redlining, and the cultural (mis)representations in the media. We hope that in working through these units students will take to heart what American educator and political activist Angela Davis said, "I am no longer accepting the things I cannot change. I am changing the things I cannot accept."

Chapter 6

Antiracism

Understanding Our History to Co-create a Better Future

Christina Thomas and Victor Antonio Lozada

Figure 6.1 **Those Who Died.** *Sofia Castilla.*

THEME AND RATIONALE

Racism is an issue that has become deeply entwined within our society, and perhaps one contributing factor is the denial that racism even exists today

(Nelson & Dunn, 2017). It is important that students consider other's perspectives in order to develop and promote a sense of awareness, empathy, and understanding (Souto-Manning & Martell, 2016; Came & Griffith, 2018). Literacy can make students aware of a history that is often not, but should be, discussed and analyzed (Saha, 2020; Rogers & Mosley, 2006), and awareness and knowledge will provide an avenue for action and change (Aouragh, 2019). Students who are unaware of varying perspectives, interpretations, and historical figures will be left ignorant in their societies and will be powerless to enact any sort of change (Noltemeyer & Grapin, 2021).

"Antiracism seeks to heal, organize and empower the oppressed, not those who are advantaged by racism and privilege" (Came & Griffith, 2018, p. 182). One of the biggest objectives of antiracism should be to bring together, not only those individuals who have been targets of racism, but also allies. Allies are people who have known privilege, yet who are willing to address and challenge the issue of racism (Came & Griffith, 2018).

In order to enact antiracism in our society, it is important that we first recognize and transparently confront prejudice and discrimination that is apparent in our educational and political systems, as well as our everyday lives (Noltemeyer & Grapin, 2021). We can achieve this purpose through "unlearning and relearning . . . [in order] to inform and spur collective action" (Came & Griffith, 2018, p. 183). Teachers must be able to accept the idea that race in and of itself is not the issue; racism is a concept perpetuated by human beings (Alemanji & Mafi, 2018).

Education on the topic of antiracism should reflect this fact and teachers should instill in their students the importance of challenging policies and power structures with inherently racist and prejudiced views and beliefs (Alemanji & Mafi, 2018). Using literacy and education, teachers can open a discussion about racial injustice, prejudice, and racism, and provide opportunities in their classroom to potentially develop strategies for growth and dialogue among students (Rogers & Mosley, 2006), creating an understanding of the prevalent inequity and imbalance of power within our society (Came & Griffith, 2018).

UNIT GOALS

Students will learn more about racism and antiracism, how racism impacts so many people's lives, how antiracism is an effective strategy for creating awareness of injustice and inequity, and how we can make changes in our society. Students will be introduced to literature regarding other's perspectives and how racism is embedded in all aspects of our society, including in the history of the United States. Students will learn how to question prejudice and discrimination when they come across it in their lives. Finally, they will learn how they can become advocates for change and equity, and be able to openly discuss and confront racism in a manner that will encourage empathy, courage, knowledge, and healing.

MULTIMODAL TEXT SET

Picture Books

- Alexander, K. (2019). *The undefeated* (K. Nelson, Illus.). Versify.
- Barnes, D. (2017). *Crown: An ode to the fresh cut* (G. C. James, Illus.). Agate Bolden.
- Cherry, M. A. (2019). *Hair love* (V. Harrison, Illus.). Kokila.
- Harrison, V. (2017). *Little leaders: Bold women in Black history*. Little, Brown Books for Young Readers.
- Higginbotham, A. (2018). *Not my idea: A book about Whiteness (Ordinary terrible things)*. Dottir Press.
- Kendi, I. X. (2020). *Antiracist baby picture book* (A. Lukashevsky, Illus.). Kokila.
- Nyong'o, L. (2019). *Sulwe* (V. Harrison, Illus.). Simon & Schuster Books for Young Readers.
- Rappaport, D. (2001). *Martin's big words: The life of Dr. Martin Luther King, Jr.* (B. Collier, Illus.). Little, Brown Books for Young Readers.
- Shabazz, I. (2014). *Malcolm Little: The boy who grew up to become Malcolm X* (A. G. Ford, Illus.). Atheneum Books for Young Readers.

Novels

- Anderson, C., & Bolden, T. (2019). *We are not yet equal: Understanding our racial divide*. Bloomsbury Children's Books.
- Bajaj, V. (2020). *Count me in*. Puffin Books.
- Celano, M. (2019). *Something happened in our town (A child's story about racial injustice)*. Magination Press.
- Cherry-Paul, S., Reynolds, J., & Kendi, I. X. (2021). *Stamped (for kids): Racism, antiracism, and you*. Little, Brown and Company.
- Coles, J. (2019). *Tyler Johnson was here*. Little, Brown Books for Young Readers.
- Elliott, Z. (2020). *Say her name (Poems to empower)* (L. Wise, Illus.). Little, Brown Books for Young Readers.
- Kendi, I. X. (2017). *Stamped from the beginning: The definitive history of racist ideas in America*. Bold Type Books.
- Kendi, I. X. (2019). *How to be an antiracist*. One World.

- Medina, T. (2017). *I am Alfonso Jones* (S. Robinson & J. Jennings, Illus.). Tu Books.
- Oshiro, M. (2019). *Anger is a gift: A novel*. Tor Teen.
- Reynolds, J., & Kendi, I. X. (2020). *Stamped: Racism, antiracism, and you: A remix of the national book award-winning Stamped from the Beginning*. Little, Brown Books for Young Readers.
- Rhodes, J. P. (2019). *Ghost boys*. Little, Brown Books for Young Readers.
- Ruffin, A., & Lamar, L. (2021). *You'll never believe what happened to Lacey: Crazy stories about racism*. Grand Central Publishing.
- Stone, N. (2018). *Dear Martin*. Ember.
- Thomas, A. (2017). *The hate you give*. Balzer and Bray.

Poetry

- Elliott, Z., & Wise, L. (2020). *Say her name*. Disney/Jump at the Sun.

Videos

- African Australian (2020, June 6). *Sesame Street explain Black Lives Matter* [Video]. YouTube. https://youtu.be/xBUFcv0y0yk
- Beyoncé. (Director). (2020). *Black is king* [Film]. Parkwood Entertainment; Walt Disney Pictures; Disney+.
- DeLoatch, M. (Executive Producer). (2019–present). *Family reunion* [TV series]. Netflix.
- Mohammad Azzam. (2013, January 4). *Robert F Kennedy announcing the death of Martin Luther King - A great speech* [Video]. YouTube. https://youtu.be/GoKzCff8Zbs
- On-Demand Entertainment (2020, June 4). *John Boyega's powerful anti-racism speech at George Floyd protest in London* [Video]. YouTube. https://youtu.be/gPV2klAQo5E
- RARE FACTS. (2017, November 7). *I have a dream speech by Martin Luther King. Jr HD (subtitled)* [Video]. YouTube. https://youtu.be/vP4iY1TtS3s
- Sony Pictures Animation (2019, December 5). *Hair love - Oscar®-winning short film (full) - Sony Pictures Animation* [Video]. YouTube. https://www.youtube.com/watch?v=kNw8V_Fkw28

Songs

- Brown, J. (1969). Say it loud - I'm Black and I'm proud [Song]. On *Say It Loud - I'm Black and I'm Proud*. King.

- Johnson, J. W., & Johnson, J. R. (2019). Lift every voice and sing [Song recorded by Beyoncé]. On *Homecoming: The Live Album*. Parkwood; Columbia (original work published 1905).
- Lamar, K., & Beyoncé. (2016). Freedom [Song]. On *Lemonade*. Parkwood; Columbia.
- Public Enemy (1989). Fight the power [Song]. On *Fear of a Black Planet*. Motown Records.

SAMPLE LESSONS

Table 6.1 illustrates how teaching this unit with the text set addresses many of the Common Core State Standards. The sample lessons mainly come from the primary shared text in the unit: *Stamped*. However, throughout the unit, teachers can bring in different texts through interactive read-alouds, viewing and discussion of videos, and independent reading from the multimodal text set.

Sample Lesson One: Understanding Our Shared History

This lesson will serve as a way to model how the class will operate with independent reading time and discussion of the novel.

Vocabulary: segregation, antiracism, assimilation
Materials:
- *Stamped* by Jason Reynolds and Ibram X. Kendi
- Vocabulary list (English, Spanish, and additional languages)
- Computers with software capable of creating multimodal presentations such as Google Slides, Prezi, or PowerPoint

Procedures:
1. Show students the short video of Ibram X. Kendi discussing antiracism, "The very heartbeat of racism is denial," which can be found on the University of Rochester's website: https://www.rochester.edu/newscenter/ibram-x-kendi-the-very-heartbeat-of-racism-is-denial-470332/. Allow time for reflection and discussion, explaining that he is one of the authors of *Stamped*, the book they will be discussing in this unit.
2. Provide students with a list of key ideas, people, and places from the Introduction to *Stamped*. (There is a list below but you may add more depending on your students' background knowledge.) In partners, have students discuss what they already know about these terms. When you return together as a class, tell students that they

Table 6.1 Unit Overview and General Teaching Ideas

Week One
- Introduction to antiracism.
- Understanding of the differences among segregation, assimilation, and antiracism.

Common Core Standards	Some Related Texts
• CCSS.ELA-LITERACY.RL.8.1 Cite the textual evidence that most strongly supports an analysis of what the text says explicitly as well as inferences drawn from the text. • CCSS.ELA-LITERACY.RH.6-8.2 Determine the central ideas or information of a primary or secondary source; provide an accurate summary of the source distinct from prior knowledge or opinions. • CCSS.ELA-LITERACY.RH.6-8.4 Determine the meaning of words and phrases as they are used in a text, including vocabulary specific to domains related to history/social studies. • CCSS.ELA-Literacy.W.8.6 Use technology, including the internet, to produce and publish writing and present the relationship between information and ideas efficiently as well as interact and collaborate with others.	• Book: *Stamped* (by Jason Reynolds and Ibram Kendi) • Book: *Stamped (for kids): Racism, antiracism, and you* (adapted by Sonja Cherry-Paul) • Book: *Stamped from the beginning: The definitive history of racist ideas in America* (by Ibram Kendi)

Weeks Two–Three
- Deepen understanding of antiracism in a variety of historical contexts including during the following time periods: 1415–1728, 1743–1826, 1826–1879, 1868–1963, and 1963–today.

Common Core Standards	Some Related Texts
• CCSS.ELA-LITERACY.RL.8.1 Cite the textual evidence that most strongly supports an analysis of what the text says explicitly as well as inferences drawn from the text. • CCSS.ELA-LITERACY.RH.6-8.2 Determine the central ideas or information of a primary or secondary source; provide an accurate summary of the source distinct from prior knowledge or opinions. • CCSS.ELA-LITERACY.RH.6-8.8 Distinguish among fact, opinion, and reasoned judgment in a text.	• Book: *Stamped* (by Jason Reynolds and Ibram Kendi) • Book: *Stamped (for kids): Racism, antiracism, and you* (adapted by Sonja Cherry-Paul) • Book: *Stamped from the beginning: The definitive history of racist ideas in America* (by Ibram Kendi)

- **Weeks Four–Five**
- Learn and discuss what racism and antiracism mean and how to apply an antiracist ideology in their lives.
- Present a product to the class that represents their interpretations from book reading using different forms of media and text.
- Discern areas relating to racism and prejudice in our society and determine social action that may be taken in order to promote empathy, knowledge, and change.

Table 6.1 Unit Overview and General Teaching Ideas (*Continued*)

Common Core Standards	Some Related Texts
• CCSS.ELA-LITERACY.RL.8.1 Cite the textual evidence that most strongly supports an analysis of what the text says explicitly as well as inferences drawn from the text. • CCSS.ELA-LITERACY.RH.6-8.2 Determine the central ideas or information of a primary or secondary source; provide an accurate summary of the source distinct from prior knowledge or opinions. • CCSS.ELA-LITERACY.RH.6-8.4 Determine the meaning of words and phrases as they are used in a text, including vocabulary specific to domains related to history/social studies.	• Book: *Stamped* (by Jason Reynolds and Ibram Kendi) • Book: *How to Be an Antiracist* • Book: *You'll Never Believe What Happened to Lacey: Crazy Stories About Racism*

will be developing definitions for some of these terms through the unit as they read *Stamped*. Ask if there are any clarification questions about the terms. It will be important they have adequate background knowledge before reading. They especially need to understand who the authors (Dr. Kendi and Mr. Reynolds) are.
- Racism
- Racist idea
- Antiracism
- Antiracist idea
- Narrative history
- Colonial America
- Jason Reynolds
- Trayvon Martin
- Darnesha Harris
- Tamir Rice
- Kimani Gray
- Michael Brown
- #BlackLivesMatter
- Racial disparities
- Racial inequities
- Thomas Jefferson
- Segregationist
- Assimilationist
- Antiracist

3. Through shared reading, read the Introduction of *Stamped* out loud while students follow along in their own copy of the book. Stop after some of the key terms to have students discuss the significance of the term.

4. Lead the students in a whole class discussion using guiding questions (e.g., What was the most relevant piece of information from what you read? What ideas, events, or people resonated with you? If you could only tell someone one piece of information from what you read, what would it be and why?). To engage more students, direct some of the questions for "turn and talk" to a partner.
5. Individually or in partners, students prepare a multimodal presentation (e.g., Google slides, PowerPoint, mural, poem, movie, song, and drama) to communicate their interpretation of the Introduction, following the rubric guidelines in Table 6.2. Explain to the students that this presentation is a reader response. They will be engaging in creating a different reader response to each of the five sections of the book.

Evaluation:
- Formative assessment: Group discussion, teacher observations, conferencing
- Summative assessment: Student presentation of their multimodal presentation

Sample Lesson Two: Transacting with Text—Reader Response Activities for Meaning-Making

Each day in class and for homework, students will independently read a chapter of *Stamped*. The teacher may also choose to read aloud certain excerpts that are particularly important or difficult to understand through shared reading. (See the Support sections for other options of student reading.) There are twenty-eight chapters divided into five sections. After reading each section of the book, each group of students selects a reader response option from the menu of activities in Table 6.3 to demonstrate their transaction with the book. Once a section is complete (and the activity has an artifact), students may share their learning with other groups. This cycle will continue for a few weeks with students continually engaged in reading and responding. Teachers should make a reading schedule so all groups are in the same section each week in order to promote whole class discussion and shared reading.

Levels: After Reading Questions/Activity

Students start at level one and "level up" when they believe they have done all of the work of the previous level.

- Level 1: What do you see in this section of *Stamped* that you have also seen in your school, home, or community?

Table 6.2 Rubric for Multimodal Presentation

	Outstanding (4)	Proficient (3)	Developing (2)	Emerging (1)
Artifact	The artifact is created in a way that conveys the author's meaning *and* shows a deep understanding of the medium.	The artifact is created in a way that *sometimes* conveys the author's meaning *and sometimes* shows a deep understanding of the medium.	The artifact is created in a way that *sometimes* conveys the author's meaning *or sometimes* shows a deep understanding of the medium.	The artifact is created in a way that *may* convey the author's meaning *or may* show a deep understanding of the medium.
Context (Rhetorical Skills)	The artifact shows deep regard for the social context in which it will be.	The artifact *often* shows deep regard for the social context in which it will be.	The artifact *sometimes* shows deep regard for the social context in which it will be.	The artifact *may* show deep regard for the social context in which it will be.
Substance	The artifact deals with the subject matter in a deep way.	The artifact *often* deals with the subject matter in a deep way.	The artifact *sometimes* deals with the subject matter in a deep way.	The artifact may deal with the subject matter in a deep way.
Process Management and Technical Skills	The student can *always* show evidence of editing.	The student can *often* show evidence of editing.	The student can *sometimes* show evidence of editing.	The student *may* be able to show evidence of editing.
Habits of Mind	The student can *always* show evidence of the use of Habits of Mind.	The student can *often* show evidence of the use of Habits of Mind.	The student can *sometimes* show evidence of Habits of Mind.	The student *may* be able to show evidence of Habits of Mind.

Note: There are many different conceptions of Habits of Mind. Wahleithner (2014) referenced the *Framework for Success in Postsecondary Writing*, which includes curiosity, openness, engagement, creativity, persistence, responsibility, flexibility, and metacognition (Council of Writing Program Administrators et al., 2011).

Table 6.3 Reader Response Menu

Levels	Always, Sometimes, or Never	Commit and Toss
Found Poem	Chant It, Sing It, Rap It	Question Gallery
Question Cube	Iconography	Random Discussion

- Level 2: Use a graphic organizer such as a Venn diagram to consider how this section of *Stamped* reflects cultural representations (labels include familiar and unfamiliar cultural representations).
- Level 3: Freewrite about what cultural representations you see in your world and the experiences you notice in the text (e.g., power, privilege, and bias).

Found Poem

Students create a found poem by finding a word, phrase, and sentence that represents their understanding of the section. Each individual student selects a word, phrase, and a sentence and writes them in their notebook. First, one-by-one, each student reads his/her sentence, then, the phrase, and finally, the word.

Question Cube (Who, What, When, Where, Why, and How)

Students use a cube labeled with questioning words to guide a small group discussion. Each side of the cube has a questioning word (who, what, when, where, why, and how) used to guide a discussion about the section. Students write questions relevant to the section of the text they read for each question word.

Always, Sometimes, or Never

Students select specific ideas from a section of the book and discuss whether they are always, sometimes, or never true. Ideas can come from previously learned vocabulary such as segregation, assimilation, and antiracism.

Chant It, Sing It, Rap It

Students discuss the main themes from the section and create a song or rap that summarizes the section of the book. See chapter 10 of this book on ways to incorporate rap using a small portion of this text.

Color, Symbol, Image

Students choose a color, create a symbol, and draw an image that represents a concept from the section of the book. Images can be posted on the wall or digitally displayed using websites such as Padlet.

Commit and Toss

Students write down questions or thoughts about the section of the book. They crumble the paper up and throw them into an empty trash bin. Students randomly grab a paper from the bin and respond to the question or thought about this section of the book.

Question Gallery

Students write questions or thoughts about each chapter that they read on sticky notes. They post the notes on the wall under each chapter heading. After students have posted the notes, everyone takes a "gallery walk" to see what ideas are presented. Small group discussion follows each chapter to understand what other people wrote or to engage with the questions posed.

Random Discussion

Students randomly select a page from their section. Students read aloud this section (no more, no less). Students discuss how this particular page reflects (or doesn't reflect) the overall ideas presented in the chapter. Repeat at least once. On the second randomly selected page, students will further the discussion by acknowledging how the two random pages connect (or don't connect) to each other.

Sample Lesson 3: Individual Inquiry into Racism

Students will become news reporters and interview two to three friends or family members. Use the following prompts and guiding questions:

- What do they know about antiracism?
- Have they or anyone they know been impacted by racism and prejudice?
- Share an excerpt from the book *Stamped*. What is their perspective on the implications of the book's overall theme?
- Would they be interested in learning more about the topic of antiracism and how can they help promote social action and change? Why or why not?

Students are encouraged to come up with their own interview questions in addition to the ones provided. Students will create a one-page newspaper based on their interviews using the following guidelines:

- One section describing demographic information regarding the people who were interviewed.
- One section featuring the excerpt from the book that you asked the interviewees to respond to.
- One section per question asked, as well as responses.
- One or more graphic representations which represent your learning and any major theme from the project which you wish to emphasize.

Figure 6.2 Peace. *John Marquez.*

Students who do not wish to create a newspaper page may demonstrate their learning using any other multimodal format such as an essay, poem, song, rap, comic strip, video, or other modes. This will be determined based on teacher discretion and individual student differentiated needs. Figure 6.2 illustrates one student's artistic representation of their learning about overcoming racism from the 1960s to the present. Table 6.4 is a rubric that teachers may use to assess students' inquiry projects.

SUPPORT FOR EMERGENT BILINGUALS

- The main text *Stamped* is available in Spanish (*Stamped: El racismo, antirracismo, y tú*). Students with a strong Spanish linguistic repertoire are encouraged to interact with the text in the language that is most comfortable for them. This helps to develop the standards more fully as they don't specify which language is needed to understand the content.
- Students should be encouraged to language in ways that foster communication including translanguaging. Lessons 1 and 2 have group discussion components. These can be done in any language(s) that is comfortable for the group. Lessons 1 and 3 have presentations. These

Table 6.4 Rubric for Individual Inquiry into Racism

Individual Inquiry into Racism Rubric	Exceeded Expectations	Met Expectations	Did Not Meet Expectations
Research	Original interview questions were used; demographic information was present; interview responses were summarized in a thoughtful manner.	Some original interview questions were used; a sincere effort was made to obtain demographic information; interview responses were summarized adequately in the presentation.	No original interview questions were used; none or minimal demographic information was present; interview responses were organized in a nonsensical manner.
Structure and Grammar	All sections were completed with color, detail, and no grammatical errors.	Most sections were completed with color, detail, and minimal grammatical errors	Several section guidelines were not met, lacking color, detail, and contained many grammatical errors.
Creative Project	The project was creative and well constructed. A substantial amount of time was spent on the idea, presentation, and thoughtfulness.	The project was well constructed. Time was spent on the idea, presentation, and thoughtfulness.	The project was not well constructed. Not much time was spent on the idea, presentation, and thoughtfulness.

can be done in any language(s) that are comfortable for the group and the audience.

SUPPORT FOR STUDENTS WITH SPECIAL LEARNING NEEDS

- Students with varying reading levels are encouraged to interact with the text in its variety of formats. For more emerging readers, *Stamped (For Kids): Racism, Antiracism, and You* adapted by Sonja Cherry-Paul may be a more appropriate way for them to interact with the text and its ideas. For more advanced readers, *Stamped from the Beginning: The Definitive History of Racist Ideas in America* by Ibram X. Kendi may be a more appropriate way for them to interact with the text and its ideas.
- For students with visual impairments, the audiobook for *Stamped* is available.

DIFFERENT GRADE LEVEL MODIFICATIONS

- To adapt this for older adolescents, consider using Kendi's original work *Stamped from the Beginning: The Definitive History of Racist Ideas in America* as the central text. Additionally, students may choose to participate in peer review of their multimodal presentations.
- To adapt for younger adolescents, consider using Sonja Cherry-Paul's adaptation of the young adult adaptation—*Stamped (For Kids): Racism, Antiracism, and You*. Additionally, some of the work could be done collaboratively among students, especially in lesson 3. Students can co-create the project rather than work individually to foster collaboration and leverage other students' strengths.

REFERENCES

Alemanji, A. A., & Mafi, B. (2018). Antiracism education? A study of an antiracism workshop in Finland. *Scandinavian Journal of Educational Research, 62*(2), 186–199. https://doi.org/10.1080/00313831.2016.1212260

Aouragh, M. (2019). 'White privilege' and shortcuts to antiracism. *Race and Class, 61*(2), 3–26. https://doi.org/10.1177/0306396819874629

Came, H., & Griffith, D. (2018). Tackling racism as a "wicked" public health problem: Enabling allies in antiracism praxis. *Social Science and Medicine, 199*, 181–188. http://doi.org/10.1016/j.socscimed.2017.03.028

Council of Writing Program Administrators, National Council of Teachers of English, & National Writing Project. (2011). *Framework for success in postsecondary writing*. Creative Commons.

Nelson, J., & Dunn, K. (2017). Neoliberal antiracism: Responding to 'everywhere but different' racism. *Progress in Human Geography, 41*(1), 26–43. https://doi.org/10.1177/0309132515627019

Noltemeyer, A., & Grapin, S. L. (2021). Working together towards social justice, antiracism, and equity: A joint commitment from school psychology international and journal of educational and psychological consultation. *School Psychology International, 42*(1), 3–10. https://doi.org/10.1177/0143034320977618

Rogers, R., & Mosley, M. (2006). Racial literacy in a second-grade classroom: Critical race theory, whiteness studies, and literacy research. *Reading Research Quarterly, 41*(4), 462–495. https://doi.org/10.1598/RRQ.41.4.3

Saha, A. (2020). The politics of representation in the politics of antiracism. *Ethnic and Racial Studies, 43*(13), 2357–2362. https://doi-org/10.1090/01419870.2020.1784453

Souto-Manning, M., & Martell, J. (2016). *Reading, writing, and talk: Inclusive teaching strategies for diverse learners, K–2*. Teachers College.

Wahleithner, J. M. (2014). The National Writing Project's Multimodal Assessment Project: Development of a framework for thinking about multimodal composing. *Computers and Compositions, 31*, 79–86. http://doi.org/10.1016/j.compcom.2013.12.004

Chapter 7

Redlining

A Mechanism of Systemic Racism

Christina Salazar

Figure 7.1 **Americana.** *Avery DeLost.*

THEME AND RATIONALE

Students in American public schools spend years learning the same narratives in history, featuring the same cast of characters. Over the last several decades, school curriculum has included a handful of women and People of Color. Often missing, however, is any discussion of oppression or marginalization, especially when analyzing current events and more recent history. This curriculum unit seeks to provide context and background to present-day racist thoughts and systematic racism by studying the specific effects of redlining and other related racist policies. This may work toward empowering students to challenge racism as they encounter it in their world.

Education, through its formative role on the citizens of our society, molds our present and our future. It, therefore, has enormous transformative potential. Wallace (2016) approaches education as a process designed to encourage children to question social norms. Therefore, the study of history should not be limited to the distant past. As I write today in the 2020s, essentially no students in K–12 classrooms are born in the 20th century. Therefore, we should approach teaching history as it relates to our students' modern lives if we wish education to fulfill its transformative potential. Further, the Common Core State standards (CCSS) have little to no analysis of redlining or systematic racism instruction. As a result, multicultural perspectives are often omitted in history textbooks (Watson-Vandiver & Wiggan, 2018).

Redlining is a practice by which People of Color are systematically denied opportunities to own property (Hinesmon-Matthews, 2010). This policy had measurable effects on modern communities and the modern wealth gap, or income disparity. As one of the clearest examples of systematic racism and its current effects, this unit centers on redlining to explain the social phenomenon of systematic racism. Through this illustrative example, we can support students in questioning other areas of racial disparity as related to systematic racism. Even among educators, there is a misconception that the effects of oppression are due to individual pathology as opposed to a systematic issue (Young, 2011). To be clear, every instance of racial disparity is an issue of racism. According to Dr. Ibram Kendi (2019; Reynolds & Kendi, 2020), no race is inherently superior or inferior to another *in any way*. Extending this logic, if we find a racial disparity we *must* assume there is a structural cause, not an intrinsic or individual cause.

Understanding systematic racism helps Students of Color recognize and resist oppression. Students will be able to use their education as a mechanism of resistance (Wallace, 2016). This is opposed to education's occasional role as a tool of assimilation. This unit will also help students from privileged groups build empathy and see oppression that might have previously been invisible. According to Applebaum (2008), those who benefit from an unjust system often do not consider their role in perpetuating it.

It is vital that students of all backgrounds learn about racist ideas and learn to question them. There is a false narrative that racism is perpetuated by a few evil individuals. This divides people into camps of racist versus not racist and evil versus good. This false narrative then makes it difficult to question the racist ideas we carry ourselves or that we encounter from people we consider to be good people. Oppression is then carried out by people who do not question the status quo (Applebaum, 2008). These insidious ideas contribute to very real and present danger to People of Color, as the 2020 murder of George Floyd reminds us. People of Color are targeted for murder because of the belief that Black is dangerous (Wallace, 2016). In order to challenge racist ideas in our classrooms, we must first confront them. Social education has long stressed the importance of continuous vigilance to accomplish the transformative potential of education (Applebaum, 2013).

UNIT GOALS

This unit will enable students to identify and question systematic racism both historically and in their modern lives. Students will understand the roots of systematic racism and racist ideas. The unit is designed for adolescents in grades 9 and 10 but includes adaptations for other grades. Included in the unit are multimodal texts and accommodations for emergent bilinguals and special populations. The primary goal of this curriculum unit is to support students in investigating racial inequalities and their potential causes as well as formulating ideas to confront systematic racism.

MULTIMODAL TEXT SET

The resources presented here are intended to support classroom exploration of topics of systemic racism and redlining. Several of these texts are included in the sample lessons while additional resources are provided for individual student projects and flexibility. There are more applications of these texts than those presented in the sample lessons. For example, any of these resources could be used to spark classroom discussion, to introduce or close a lesson, or to provide additional resources for students who are working ahead of schedule or who would like to explore the issues further. Another possibility is providing selection opportunities of particular texts to different students, differentiated based on strengths and interests, and asking students to present their learning to the class or a group. Teachers can include a choice board of presentation options to reflect students' strengths and comfort. For example, some students may be very comfortable speaking in front of groups while others would rather create a website to share their findings. As classroom experts, instructors should not feel limited to the suggested uses in this chapter.

Picture Books

- Alexander, K., & Nelson, K. (2020). *The undefeated*. Andersen Press.
- Nelson, V. M., & Bootman, C. (2006). *Almost to freedom*. Carolrhoda Books.
- Rappaport, D. (2007). *Martin's big words*. Little, Brown Books for Young Readers.

Videos

- Barbie (2020, October 7). *Barbie and Nikki Discuss Racism.* YouTube. https://www.youtube.com/watch?v=RCzwoMDgF_I
- CollegeHumor (2017, October 4). *The disturbing history of the suburbs - Adam ruins everything* [Video]. YouTube. https://www.youtube.com/watch?v=ETR9qrVS17g
- Films Media Group (1994). Dr. Martin Luther King Jr. The Dream. *Learn360*. https://learn360.infobase.com/PortalPlaylists.aspx?wID=114511&xtid=183596
- Films Media Group (2001). Franklin Delano Roosevelt. *Learn360*. https://learn360.infobase.com/PortalPlaylists.aspx?wID=114511&xtid=83780
- Films Media Group (2003). The gilded age. *Learn360*. https://learn360.infobase.com/PortalPlaylists.aspx?wID=114511&xtid=154909
- NPR (2018, April 11). *Housing segregation and redlining in America: A short history - Code switch - NPR* [Video]. YouTube. https://www.youtube.com/watch?v=O5FBJyqfoLM&ab_channel=NPR

Reference Sources

- Fair Housing Act (2020). In *Encyclopædia Britannica*. Retrieved from https://school.eb.com/levels/elementary/article/Fair-Housing-Act/632867

Chapter Books

- Kendi, I. X., & Reynolds, J. (2020). *Stamped: Racism, antiracism, and you*. Little, Brown and Company.
- Loewen, J. W. (2006). *Sundown towns: A hidden dimension of American racism*. Touchstone.

Informational Articles

- Nelson, R. K. Mapping Inequality. *Digital Scholarship Lab*. https://dsl.richmond.edu/panorama/redlining/
- Powell, M. (2009). Bank Accused of Pushing Mortgage Deals on Blacks. *New York Times*.
- *7 Steps to Addressing the Post-Racial Myth*. Power Poetry. https://powerpoetry.org/actions/7-steps-addressing-post-racial-myth

Images

- Temple, K. Signing of the Housing and Urban Development Act. LBJ Presidential Library. Comic strip, The New Orleans Times-Picayune. https://www.lbjlibrary.org/object/physical-artifact/signing-housing-and-urban-development-act-0

Interactive Sites

- Cheney, M. Sundown Towns in the United States. https://sundown.tougaloo.edu/content.php?file=sundowntowns-whitemap.html
- Digital Scholarship Lab, "Renewing Inequality," *American Panorama*, ed. Robert K. Nelson and Edward L. Ayers, accessed November 24, 2020, https://dsl.richmond.edu/panorama/renewal/.
- Lamster, M. (2020, September 23). Reckoning With Joppa. https://interactives.dallasnews.com/2020/historic-freedmans-town-joppa-confronts-history-racism-neglect-dallas
- Rhynhart, R. (2020). Mapping the Legacy of Structural Racism in Philadelphia - Office of the Controller. https://controller.phila.gov/philadelphia-audits/mapping-the-legacy-of-structural-racism-in-philadelphia/

SAMPLE LESSONS

There are various teaching ideas for this unit outlined in Table 7.1. All sample lessons follow the standards in the table.

Talk Read Talk Write (TRTW) is an instructional activity further developed in the book *Talk, Read, Talk, Write* by Nancy Motley (2016). It is a method for implementing structured conversation, reading, and writing throughout the curriculum. These lessons follow the TRTW format to introduce classroom discussion and thinking about racism and its roots in the United States.

Sample Lesson One: Introduction to Racism

This is an appropropriate lesson to begin the entire unit on redlining. Students will understand what redlining is, connect it to systemic racism and Jim Crow laws. They will apply this to present-day situations.

Talk—Is Racism a Problem Today? How Do You Know?

Students begin by answering this prompt individually, then, after students have had time to consider the question and formulate a response, they are directed to discuss with a classmate using any classroom conversation strategy like *Turn and Talk* with a partner or *Table Talk* with those in their group.

Table 7.1 Unit Overview and General Teaching Ideas

Week One
- Origin of racist ideas
  - Zurara
  - Nathaniel Bacon revolution
- Roots of U.S. systematic racism
  - Slavery
  - Jim Crow

Common Core Standards	Some Related Texts
• CCSS.ELA-LITERACY.RH.9-10.2 Determine the central ideas or information of a primary or secondary source; provide an accurate summary of how key events or ideas develop over the course of the text. • CCSS.ELA-LITERACY.RH.9-10.3 Analyze in detail a series of events described in a text; determine whether earlier events caused later ones or simply preceded them. • CCSS.ELA-LITERACY.RH.9-10.10 By the end of grade 10, read and comprehend history/social studies texts in grades 9–10 text complexity band independently and proficiently.	• *Stamped* • Films Media Group (2003). The gilded age. *Learn360*. https://learn360.infobase.com/PortalPlaylists.aspx?wID=114511&xtid=154909 • Nelson, V. M., & Bootman, C. (2006). *Almost to freedom*. Carolrhoda Books.

Week Two
- Definition of systematic racism.
- FDR—New Deal
- Definition of Redlining
- Lasting economic impacts of redlining

Common Core Standards	Some Related Texts
• CCSS.ELA-LITERACY.RH.9-10.2 Determine the central ideas or information of a primary or secondary source; provide an accurate summary of how key events or ideas develop over the course of the text. • CCSS.ELA-LITERACY.RH.9-10.3 Analyze in detail a series of events described in a text; determine whether earlier events caused later ones or simply preceded them. • CCSS.ELA-LITERACY.RH.9-10.10 By the end of grade 10, read and comprehend history/social studies texts in the grades 9–10 text complexity band independently and proficiently.	• Cheney, M. Sundown Towns in the United States. https://sundown.tougaloo.edu/content.php?file=sundowntowns-whitemap.html • Lamster, M. (2020, September 23). Reckoning With Joppa. https://interactives.dallasnews.com/2020/historic-freedmans-town-joppa-confronts-history-racism-neglect-dallas • Films Media Group. (2001). Franklin Delano Roosevelt. *Learn360*. https://learn360.infobase.com/PortalPlaylists.aspx?wID=114511&xtid=83780 • CollegeHumor. (2017, October 4). *The disturbing history of the suburbs - Adam ruins everything* [Video]. YouTube. https://www.youtube.com/watch?v=ETR9qrVS17g

Week Three
- Civil Rights Movement
- MLK and Malcolm X
- MLK's death
- Civil Rights Act

Common Core Standards	Some Related Texts
• CCSS.ELA-LITERACY.RH.9-10.2 Determine the central ideas or information of a primary or secondary source; provide an accurate summary of how key events or ideas develop over the course of the text. • CCSS.ELA-LITERACY.RH.9-10.3 Analyze in detail a series of events described in a text; determine whether earlier events caused later ones or simply preceded them. • CCSS.ELA-LITERACY.RH.9-10.10 By the end of grade 10, read and comprehend history/social studies texts in the grades 9–10 text complexity band independently and proficiently.	• Fair Housing Act. (2020). In Encyclopaedia Britannica. Retrieved from https://school.eb.com/levels/elementary/article/Fair-Housing-Act/632867 • Rappaport, D. (2007). *Martin's big words*. Little, Brown Books for Young Readers. • Alexander, K., & Nelson, K. (2020). *The undefeated*. Andersen Press.

(Continued)

Table 7.1 Unit Overview and General Teaching Ideas *(Continued)*

Week Four
- Present-day housing discrimination.
- Brief overview of modern issues in systematic racism
    - In education
    - Prison system
    - Police brutality
    - Medicine
    - Police brutality, etc.
- Inquiry Project

Common Core Standards	Some Related Texts
• CCSS.ELA-LITERACY.RH.9-10.2 Determine the central ideas or information of a primary or secondary source; provide an accurate summary of how key events or ideas develop over the course of the text. • CCSS.ELA-LITERACY.RH.9-10.3 Analyze in detail a series of events described in a text; determine whether earlier events caused later ones or simply preceded them. • CCSS.ELA-LITERACY.RH.9-10.10 By the end of grade 10, read and comprehend history/social studies texts in the grades 9–10 text complexity band independently and proficiently. • CCSS.ELA-LITERACY.RH.9-10.1 Cite specific textual evidence to support analysis of primary and secondary sources, attending to such features as the date and origin of the information.	• Powell, M. (2009). Bank Accused of Pushing Mortgage Deals on Blacks. *New York Times*. • *7 Steps to Addressing the Post-Racial Myth*. Power Poetry. https://powerpoetry.org/actions/7-steps-addressing-post-racial-myth

Read—Almost to Freedom, Picture Book by Nelson and Bootman.

Students can read this book through a teacher-directed whole class interactive read-aloud, shared reading by the teaching reading aloud while projecting the book on a screen, independently, or in pairs when enough copies are available.

Talk—Once the Slaves Were Free, Were Black People Free?
How Do You Know? Are Black People Free Now?

Allow students time to formulate their own ideas and write them down before implementing classroom discussion strategies.

Watch—African Americans during the Gilded Age

This is a short clip from a longer documentary about the Gilded Age. It begins with the implementation of Jim Crow laws throughout the South. Other videos, books, or media that describe the origination of Jim Crow are also appropriate.

Write—What Motivated the Creation of Jim Crow Laws?
How Do These Policies Affect People Today?

At the end of this lesson, students should address the prompt above in their writer's notebooks (digital or composition notebooks). Students can read their writing into a video recording software to encourage editing of their writing. Sentence stems will help emergent bilinguals and reluctant writers: I think that _____ motivated the creation of Jim Crow laws because _____. People created Jim Crow laws because _____. These policies affect people today by _____.

Extension—Redlining Monopoly

Play Monopoly in groups of three to four. The rules stay the same except that some students, chosen at random, will start with less money and be forbidden from buying property on the more expensive parts of the board. Students record the final amount of money held by each student at the end of the game. If time allows, there should be classroom discussion about how it feels to play Monopoly this way, how fair this game is, and how it relates to the study of racism in the United States.

Sample Lesson Two: FDR's New Deal and Redlining

In this lesson, students will learn about redlining, what it is, and its origins, and begin to consider the wider social impacts of such a policy. Students will begin the lesson by reflecting on the Monopoly game played at the end of the previous class. The class will watch a short video detailing the New Deal from the Learn 360 website. Other books or media which cover the same information can be substituted.

Watch—FDR's New Deal

https://learn360.infobase.com/PortalPlaylists.aspx?wID=114511&xtid=83780&loid=348448

Talk—Why Did the U.S. Government Feel the Need to Come Up with This New Deal? Was Everyone Benefitted? Equally?

After watching the clip, allow time for students to formulate their own ideas about the following prompt and write them down before classroom discussion strategies are implemented. I recommend varying the classroom discussion strategies to keep students engaged.

Look—Philadelphia Redlining Map, Found in the Text Set (Ryynhard, 2020)

Make color copies or project/display the map for the whole class. Students need to be given some time to think about what they notice about the map.

Talk—What Do You Notice about These Maps? What Do You Think Is Represented by the Different Colors?

Students formulate their own ideas about the following prompt and write them down before classroom discussion strategies are implemented. It is particularly important that students are prompted to notice anything without wrong or right answers. Students will be more likely to participate if stakes are low.

Direct Teach—Explain What Redlining Is.

The teacher provides direct instruction to provide a definition of and explanation of redlining. This should not take longer than 10 minutes, though less time may be required.

Talk—Why Do You Think People Did Not Just Move to Green Areas?

Allow students time to formulate their own ideas about the prompt and write them down before classroom discussion strategies are implemented. Remind students that all thinking and ideas are encouraged.

Look—Levitt (Levittown Standard Lease, Clause 25, 1947), Found in Sundown Towns: A Hidden Dimension of American Racism.

Depending on student strength in reading complex language, the teacher may need to offer significant support for reading this lease. It may be appropriate for the teacher to read the lease to the class. If the teacher reads the lease aloud, they should be sure to model the thinking and approach they take with complex texts in order to provide students with the scaffolding to independently approach future texts.

Talk—What Does This (the Lease) Mean? So If People Can't Move or Get Money_____

Allow students time to formulate their own ideas from the prompt and write them down before classroom discussion strategies are implemented. I recommend varying the classroom discussion strategies to keep students engaged.

Play—Monopoly with the Same Money as Leftover Yesterday.

Students play Monopoly with the same groups and rules as the previous day. Students all receive an initial $200 to simulate passing go but should otherwise play with the amount of money with which they ended the previous lesson. Again, students should keep a record of final dollar amounts.

Talk—Did the Game Go Faster or Slower Today? Why? Why Do You Think I Picked These Rules Today? What Does This Represent? How Is This Related to the Redlining We've Been Talking About?

Again, allow students time to formulate their own ideas about the prompts and write them down before classroom discussion begins. Encourage all thinking and discussions. Consider implementing anonymous responses, using software or posting forums to lower stakes.

Direct Teach—Redlining Plus Jim Crow Led to the Civil Rights Movement

This direct teaching should be very short, approximately five minutes, but allow students to bridge the learning of the two previous days.

Read—Martin's Big Words

The instructor conducts a whole group read-aloud of the aforementioned picture book. YouTube read-alouds are not recommended because a live, interactive read-aloud by the teacher will be more engaging and the teacher can gauge student comprehension to know when to pause for clarification, slow down, or engage in discussion.

Exit Ticket—Draw a Picture Response to This Book on a Post-It; Post It on the Wall.

Give all students a post-it to create a visual response to the picture book. They can post their responses in a designated area as they leave the room.

Sample Lesson Three: Modern Iterations of Systemic Racism

In this final lesson before beginning the inquiry unit, students consider the Civil Rights Movement, Civil Rights Act of 1964 and modern iterations of systemic racism.

Watch—Reaction to MLK Death, Video Provided in the Multimodal Text Set.

Students watch this very moving clip of the reaction to Martin Luther King's death in order to begin to understand how his death sparked support for the passing of the Civil Rights Act.

Talk—How Does This Make You Feel? How Do You Think People at the Time Felt?

This discussion prompt is somewhat visceral and some students may not wish to respond. The teacher may mitigate this by holding a whole class discussion and allowing students who volunteer to discuss or by making this a written response without a conversation component.

Read—Fair Housing Act. (2020). In Encyclopædia Britannica. Retrieved from https://school.eb.com/levels/elementary/article/Fair-Housing-Act/632867

This article from Britannica has significant support for students including varying reading levels and options for the text to be read to students. Often Britannica will have Spanish-language articles under Britannica Escolar. Ask your school librarian about access to Britannica and other online encyclopedias.

Look—Johnson Talking to FDR Cartoon, Provided in the Multimodal Text Set.

The cartoon refers to LBJ making FDR's New Deal more fair by signing the Civil Rights Act. The cartoon holds FDR in reverence. Students will use the cartoon and encyclopedia to create a mindmap.

Brainstorm—Create a Mindmap with a Partner Explaining the Fair Housing Act. Include Why It Was Enacted and What It Did. Include Connections to the Political Cartoon.

Instructors decide whether or not groups should be self-selected or instructor-determined on a class-to-class basis. Remind students that any ideas are encouraged on the mindmap.

Play—Monopoly, Remove Segregation but Keep Money from Last Game

Students play Monopoly again, but this time, segregation will be removed as a factor. In this round, students can purchase property on any part of the board. However, financial standing should not change. Again, students will begin with $200 in addition to whatever money they had leftover from the last game. This will be analogous to the lasting effects of redlining and segregation.

Talk—Now That We Have Removed Segregation, Was This Finally a Fair Game? Why or Why Not?

This discussion prompt may take less processing time and pre-writing responses may not be necessary.

Watch—Adam Explains Everything; Link Provided in the Multimodal Text Set.

This YouTube video is very effective for explaining the lasting effects of redlining and tying together the unit before the inquiry project begins.

Read—New York Times Article, "Bank Accused of Pushing Mortgage Deals on Blacks," in the Multimodal Text Set.

Encourage students to read this article individually though the teacher may choose to scaffold the reading as necessary. For example, the teacher can provide instruction in accessing more complex texts like instructing students in finding topic sentences in each paragraph and creating an outline of key ideas.

Talk—What Does This Article Tell Us about Systematic Racism Today? (Padlet)

The classroom discussion website Padlet is suggested but the instructor may choose to substitute Paldet for any classroom discussion technique that they have found effective.

Read—The Undefeated, Picture Book

The Undefeated is an incredibly moving poem turned picture book. Use a document camera, ebook, or similar technology so that all students see the images well. There are also read-alouds of the texts available online but in-person reading will often be more effective and poignant.

Brainstorm—With Your Partner, Come Up with as Many Current Issues in Racism as You Can.

Compile class ideas (using Padlet or something similar) Again, students should be encouraged to share all ideas and no ideas should be considered incorrect unless they negate the experiences of the People of Color.

Brainstorm—Pick an Issue with Your Partner and Come Up with Ways to Solve It.

Students look through the class compilation of ideas and discuss/determine their focus for the inquiry project. After choosing an issue to focus on for the inquiry project, students brainstorm all possible solutions and improvements.

GUIDELINES FOR A STUDENT INDIVIDUAL INQUIRY PROJECT

The purpose of the individual inquiry project is to apply the unit's learning about systematic racism to current events and issues. Teachers will provide options for research for current issues in racism: racism in education, police brutality, housing discrimination, food deserts, Black Lives Matter, and so on. Students are not limited to these topics. Provide students instruction on reliable sources so they can gather information from those sources. After gathering information, students will synthesize findings and determine main ideas and conclusions. Students will brainstorm possible solutions and remedies for their researched topics. Finally, students will produce a multimodal text to present their findings and ideas. Multimodal options include but are not limited to writing a children's book, creating a pamphlet, making a video, or creating a slideshow. Table 7.2 is a rubric teachers may use to evaluate student learning during the inquiry project.

SUPPORT FOR EMERGENT BILINGUALS

- Use visuals when teaching about abstract concepts. You can search for images that will help bring your teaching to life and display them while you teach.

Table 7.2 Evaluation Criteria for Multimodal Inquiry Project

Criteria	Details	Points
Norms	• Spelling • Grammar • Neatness • Punctuation	20
Research	• Use of reliable sources • Completeness of information (no significant gaps in time frames, regions, etc.) • Citations	35
Presentation of findings/ideas	• Clarity of presentation • Thoroughness (no significant gaps between information gathered and findings) • Synthesis of information (new conclusions/ thoughts drawn from information) • Ideas for remedies and solutions	45

- Provide students the option to research in their home language in addition to English. They might find rich information they can better comprehend in their language.
- Use sentence stems for writing portions of the unit.

SUPPORT FOR STUDENTS WITH SPECIAL LEARNING NEEDS

- Many of the books and articles have audio recordings. Students can listen while they are reading for comprehension support.
- Numerous multimodal options are possible for students to share their learning in the final project. Work with specialists in your school as well as with each individual student to determine the best way for them to express their learning through visuals, text, speech, movement, video, art, or other modes.
- Work with your school librarian to curate a text set that will meet the needs of all learners in your classroom.

TEACHING A MODIFIED UNIT FOR UPPER ELEMENTARY

Modify this unit for elementary grades to introduce racism and systemic racism to upper-elementary-aged students. First, read *The Undefeated*, by Kwame Alexander. Students then discuss the following questions with a partner:

1. What do you think that book was about?
2. How did the book make you feel?

Students may respond on a Google slide, introducing a possible format for the final inquiry project. Then students view an alternate text, such as the Barbie video in the Multimodal Text Set, explaining racism to a younger demographic, and respond in a manner as in Figure 7.2. Determine whether to provide background information before the initial read-aloud of *The Undefeated*. Providing background information will support some readers in making connections with the text while skipping background information can be used to evaluate students' background knowledge on racism. When I taught this lesson, I became emotional and chose to explain my response to the student.

Figure 7.2 Student work. *Natalia Salazar.*

REFERENCES

Applebaum, B. (2008). White privilege/white complicity: Connecting "benefiting from" to "contributing to." *Philosophy of Education Yearbook*, 292–300.

Hinesmon-Matthews, L. J. (2010). Redlining. In L. M. Alexander & W. C. Rucker (Eds.), *Encyclopedia of African American history* (Vol. 3, pp. 985–986). ABC-CLIO. https://link.gale.com/apps/doc/CX2442300608/GVRL?u=txshracd2583&sid=GVRL&xid=1a112ddd

Kendi, I. X. (2019). *How to be an antiracist* (1st ed.). One World.

Motley, N. (2016). *Talk read talk write*. Seidlitz Education.

Reynolds, J. (2020). *Stamped*. Little, Brown and Company.

Wallace, D. M. (2016). Liberation through education: Teaching #BlackLivesMatter in Africana studies. *Radical Teacher*, 106, 29–39. https://doi.org/10.5195/rt.2016.308

Watson-Vandiver, M. J., & Wiggan, G. (2018). The genius of Imhotep: An exploration of African-centered curricula and teaching in a high achieving U.S. urban school. *Teaching and Teacher Education,* 76, 151–164. http://dx.doi.org/10.1016/j.tate.2018.09.001

Young, E. Y. (2011). The four personae of racism: Educators' (mis)understanding of individual vs. systemic racism. *Urban Education, 46*(6), 1433–1460.

Chapter 8

Cultural (Mis)representations in the Media

Challenging Hegemonic Ideas

Phyliciá Anderson

Figure 8.1 Striving for Equality. *Eden Carty.*

THEME AND RATIONALE

The Eurocentric ideas often presented to students through various genres of art, music, film, and literature when studying the history of the United States and various topics therein has led to a misunderstanding among the various cultures represented in the United States. These misrepresentations often fuel hate and lead to what can be referred to as racist ideas (Reynolds & Kendi, 2020) as it is human nature to shy away from what is not understood, or what is often misunderstood. When adolescent literacy focuses on navigating the identity of our students, their culture, and the powers that help or hinder their success (Moje et al., 2017), students develop the tools needed to communicate successfully across multiple cultures as they work to tear down stereotypes and build a culture of appreciation.

In order to build cultures of appreciation, educators must recognize the many identities students bring with them into the classroom (Love, 2019). This includes the recognition of intersections within race, class, gender, sexuality, and social histories within youth media and pop culture (Haddix et al., 2017). However, with this recognition of intersectionality is a need to recognize the sometimes negative stereotypes that form the opinions about various groups and communities and the role of the media in perpetuating these stereotypes.

Since representations of marginalized populations are often portrayed in the media inaccurately and usually do not represent the values and ideas within that specified culture, it is important for future generations to be educated on how many cultures in the United States have been misrepresented throughout history (Wynter-Hoyte & Smith, 2020) and the impact these misrepresentations have had on society.

Taking a critical lens to the various genres of art, music, film, and literature will allow students to analyze multiple perspectives and ideas surrounding these topics and draw their own conclusions about the impact of media when portraying historical events. Through this pedagogy of freedom (Freire, 1998), students will develop a sense of cultural pride and identity while also receiving the tools to become change agents within their communities. Thus, as students learn to be critical viewers of the media, they learn the skills necessary to build a more just society.

UNIT GOALS

Throughout this unit, students will analyze and understand the impact the media has had on cultural representations and the development of various forms of stereotyping often portrayed in societal interactions. The text set includes multiple forms of literacy that can be used to assist in the academic achievement of diverse learners from varying cultural backgrounds, abilities, and at varying grade levels. Through text exploration, students will be encouraged to do the work of the abolitionist by learning to fight against injustices while understanding the powers that may be working against individuals within their community. By the end of this unit, students will be able to articulate their understanding of the impact the media has played in the development of the American culture by offering varying perspectives used when synthesizing their ideas to a determining conclusion.

MULTIMODAL TEXT SET

This text set is only a jumping-off place for you to build your own text set for your specific student population. Every month there are more children's, adolescents', and YA books published about this topic and there are continually more articles and multimedia resources as well. Stay informed by subscribing to Learning for Justice (https://www.learningforjustice.org/) and participating in organizations such as the National Council for Teachers of English Build Your Stack (https://ncte.org/build-your-stack/), which helps teachers gain knowledge on growing their classroom libraries.

Picture Books

- Nagara, I. (2016). *A is for activist*. Seven Stories Press.
- Browne, M. L., Acevedo, E., & Gatwood, O. (2020). *Woke: A young poet's call to justice*. Roaring Brook Press.

Artwork

- Beam Imagination. (2019, February 1). *Off the wall Atlanta*. [Video]. YouTube. https://youtu.be/cnJouTkZmCU
- Yadav, N. (2017). *ABC of social issues*. Behance. infographic, Bangalore, India; Adobe. https://www.behance.net/gallery/46957323/ABC-of-Social-Issues-Adobes-Project1324

Audio and Visual

- Cut. (2015, September 11). *America | around the world - Ep 4 | Cut*. [Video]. YouTube. https://youtu.be/iCap6I9MlOw
- Jeremy. (2018, April 30). *Pop music around the world*. [Video]. YouTube. https://youtu.be/lPEDP-lMvNI

- University of Michigan College of Literature, Science, and the Arts. (2013, August 29). *American culture: Global perspective.* [Video]. YouTube. https://youtu.be/3M1T_22vuPk

Websites

- Brave New Voices. (2020). *Brave new voices: International youth poetry festival.* https://bnv20.youthspeaks.org
- News18. (2020). *In Photos | 20 protests making headlines around the world in 2020.* https://www.news18.com/photogallery/world/in-photos-20-protests-making-headlines-around-the-world-in-2020-2931535.html
- NPR. (2021). *What the world listened to most in 2016.* https://www.npr.org/sections/therecord/2017/04/26/525609365/what-the-world-listened-to-most-in-2016
- StoryCorps, Inc. (2021). *The StoryCorps podcast.* https://storycorps.org/podcast

Informational Articles

- Cismas, S. C. (2010). The impact of American culture on other cultures: Language and cultural identity. In L. A. Zadeh, J. Kacprzyk, N. Mastorakis, A. Kuri-Morales, P. Borne, & L. Kazovsky (Eds.), *Recent advances in artificial intelligence, knowledge engineering, and data bases: Proceedings of the 9th WSEAS International Conference on Artificial Intelligence, Knowledge Engineering and Data Bases* (pp. 388–393). Essay, WSEAS. http://www.wseas.us/e-library/conferences/2010/Cambridge/AIKED/AIKED-61.pdf
- Diamond, A. (2020, March 4). How women broke into the male-dominated world of cartoons and illustrations. *Tween Tribune.* https://www.tweentribune.com/article/teen/how-women-broke-male-dominated-world-cartoons-and-illustrations/
- Katz, B. (2019, September 20). A new Monopoly celebrates women. But what about the game's own overlooked inventor? *Tween Tribune.* https://www.tweentribune.com/article/teen/new-monopoly-celebrates-women-what-about-games-own-overlooked-inventor/
- Recker, J. (2019, April 25). How the music of Hawaii's last ruler guided the Island's people through crisis. *Tween Tribune.* https://www.tweentribune.com/article/teen/how-music-hawaiis-last-ruler-guided-islands-people-through-crisis/
- Science Monitor, C. (2020, September 23). How video games are teaching the world to speak English. *Newsela.* https://newsela.com/read/video-games-teaching-english/id/2001013780/?search_id=85dfd2c8-334e-4ba1-bb5d-9a5987e44cd4

SAMPLE LESSONS

The sample lessons come from the teaching ideas and standards in Table 8.1. Teachers can use the text set in order to create unique lessons for this unit to meet the needs of their diverse student populations.

Sample Lesson One: Choosing an Issue

Learning Target:
- Students will evaluate multiple sources of information presented in diverse formats.

Resources:
- Video: American Culture. Global Perspective
- *A is for Activist* by Innosanto Nagara
- Infographic: "ABC of Social Issues" by Niteesh Yadav

Procedures:
1. Begin by introducing the unit question students will be looking to determine throughout the week: How have issues in the United States been reflected in the media?
2. Then, show students the video: American Culture. Global Perspective. As students watch the video they should think about the impact the American culture has on society.
3. Discuss a key takeaway from the video.
4. Next, ask students to get in small groups and read the book *A is for Activist* by Innosanto Nagara.
5. After reading, students should work together to select a color, create a symbol, and draw an image that represents one of the letters in the book.
6. They can use a large sticky poster or digital platform to create their color, symbol, and image.
7. Finally, ask students to review the Infographic: "ABC of Social Issues" by Niteesh Yadav and choose a social issue to track throughout the unit.
8. Students can share their findings by answering the questions on the Choosing a Social Issue assessment.

Assessment: Choosing a Social Issue:
1. Where have you noticed this issue in your school, home, or community?
2. Where have you seen this issue represented in the world?
3. What are some major debates or concerns within this issue?

Figure 8.2 represents an artistic representation from a social issue students might select.

Table 8.1   Unit Overview and General Teaching Ideas

Weeks One–Two
- Issues through the Arts
- How have issues in the United States been reflected in the media?
- Issues in the United States during the following centuries:
  - 1870s, 1880s, and 1890s
  - 1900s, 1910s, 1920s, 1930s, 1940s, 1950s, 1960s, 1970s, 1980s, and 1990s
  - 2000s, 2010s, and 2020

Common Core Standards	Some Related Texts
• CCSS.ELA-LITERACY.RH.11-12.7 Integrate and evaluate multiple sources of information presented in diverse formats and media (e.g., visually, quantitatively, as well as in words) in order to address a question or solve a problem.	• American Culture. Global Perspective • How women broke into the male-dominated world of cartoons and illustrations • ABC of Social Issues • Story Corps • *A is for Activist* by Innosanto Nagara

Weeks Three–Four
- Cultural Movements
- What impact did this issue have on cultural movements in art, music, and literature?
- Sample Movements:
  - Harlem Renaissance
  - Rock and Roll
  - Chicano Murals
  - War on Terror
  - Black Power
  - Dreamers/DACA

Common Core Standards	Some Related Texts
• CCSS.ELA-LITERACY.RH.11-12.8 Evaluate an author's premises, claims, and evidence by corroborating or challenging them with other information.	• Off The Wall Atlanta by Beam Imagination • "How the music of Hawaii's last ruler guided the Island's people through crisis" by Jane Recker • Brave New Voices • "A new Monopoly celebrates women. But what about the game's own overlooked inventor?" by Brigit Katz

Weeks Five–Six
- Spread of american culture
- How were art, music, and literature used to spread information about the American culture around the world?
- Global dissemination
- Protests
- Representation
- Stereotypes

Cultural (Mis)representations in the Media 127

Table 8.1 Unit Overview and General Teaching Ideas (Continued)

Common Core Standards	Some Related Texts
• CCSS.ELA-LITERACY.RH.11-12.9 Integrate information from diverse sources, both primary and secondary, into a coherent understanding of an idea or event, noting discrepancies among sources.	• America | Around the World - Ep 4 | Cut • What The World Listened To Most In 2016 • Pop Music Around The World • How video games are teaching the world to speak English • The impact of American culture on other cultures: Language and cultural identity • In Photos | 20 Protests Making Headlines Around the World in 2020

Sample Lesson Two: Asking the Harder Questions

Figure 8.2 A Fight for a Basic Right. *Tieryan Quintero.*

Learning Target:
- Students will evaluate an author's premises, claims, and evidence by corroborating or challenging them with other information.

Resources:
- Brave New Voices

Procedures:
1. Review the unit question students have been considering throughout the week: What impact did this issue have on cultural movements in art, music, and literature?
2. Ask students to use the Brave New Voices, or another resource to find a spoken word video that relates to their issue.
3. After viewing their video, ask students to respond in the form of a Commit and Toss by writing the following on a piece of paper:
    a. Quote a line from the spoken word video that stood out to you the most. This may be positive or negative but should give your classmates something to think about.
    b. Respond to that line by asking a question or by making a statement.
    c. DO NOT write your name on the paper.
    d. Save some space for another classmate to respond.
4. Next, ask students to crumble the paper and toss it in the (empty) trash, bin, basket, container, etc.
5. After all students have tossed their response, all students can then take turns grabbing a paper that has been tossed (hopefully not their own).
6. Students should then read the quoted line, question, or statement and then respond with an answer, another statement, another question, etc.
7. Depending on the class size, students can repeat steps 4–6 at the teacher's discretion.
8. After the last student responds to the paper they have received, each student should take turns standing and reciting what their paper says.
9. After presenting, students can finish the lesson by completing the "How I am feeling? What I am Thinking?" assessment.

Assessment: How I Am Feeling? What I Am Thinking?
- Students get a sticky note to share their ideas about what they heard concerning their issue by telling how they are feeling or what they are thinking.
- The sticky notes can then be posted on the wall.

GUIDELINES FOR A STUDENT INQUIRY PROJECT

The student inquiry project will take many class periods and will build on knowledge students have gained in the first part of the unit. They will have the opportunity to further investigate a particular era they are interested in and would like to know more about. During the class periods designated for the student inquiry project, the teacher may still conduct mini-lessons on particular areas of how to conduct research or elements of writing that will guide the students as they independently research and complete their projects. Table 8.2 is a rubric to assess student learning during the inquiry project part of the unit. Students may also use the rubric to guide them as they work on their projects.

Learning Targets

- Students will understand the relationship between the arts and the times during which they were created.
- Students will use class time throughout the unit to work on their inquiry project. Throughout the unit, students are seeking to determine how historical events have been represented in the media.
- Students should begin the project by choosing an issue within one of the following decades. As the unit progresses, they will determine how that issue has been represented in the media.
  - 1870s, 1880s, and 1890s
  - 1900s, 1910s, 1920s, 1930s, 1940s, 1950s, 1960s, 1970s, 1980s, and 1990s
  - 2000s, 2010s, and 2020s

After researching the media representation of their issue, students will use the remaining weeks to create a One-Page Newspaper (using a digital platform) about what they have learned:

- **Section 1:** What major issue is taking place during this time in history?
- **Section 2:** How has this major issue been reflected in the media? (This could be shown through art, music, film, literature, or all of the above.)
- **Section 3:** Describe a cultural movement that came because of this issue and the form(s) of media that were used to impact the American society.
- **Section 4:** Analyze the impact the representation of this issue in the media had on cultural stereotypes. Be sure to include multiple perspectives.

Table 8.2 Media Representation Student Inquiry Project Rubric

Skill	Great Job (20-16)	Almost There (15-11)	Not There (10-0)	Total Points
Section 1: Major Issue in History	The student describes the characteristics of a major issue in U.S. history.	The student somewhat describes the characteristics of a major issue in U.S. history.	The student does not describe the characteristics of a major issue in U.S. history.	20
Section 2: Reflections in the Media	The student describes how a major issue was reflected in various genres of art, music, film, and literature—the media.	The student somewhat describes how a major issue was reflected in various genres of art, music, film, and literature—the media.	The student does not describe how a major issue was reflected in various genres of art, music, film, and literature—the media.	20
Section 3: Impact on Society	The student describes the impact media representations concerning this issue had on the American society.	The student somewhat describes the impact media representations concerning this issue had on the American society.	The student does not describe the impact media representations concerning this issue had on the American society.	20
Section 4: Global Diffusion	The student identifies and analyzes stereotypes concerning the American culture that developed as a result of the media representation concerning this issue.	The student somewhat identifies or analyzes stereotypes concerning the American culture that developed as a result of the media representation concerning this issue.	The student does not identify or analyze stereotypes concerning the American culture that developed as a result of the media representation concerning this issue.	20
Aesthetics	All squares are neatly completed with color and detail.	Most squares are neatly completed with color or detail.	No squares are neatly completed with color or detail.	10
Conventions	Grammar, spelling, and punctuation make it easy to understand ideas.	Grammar, spelling, and punctuation lead to confusion when understanding some ideas.	Grammar, spelling, and punctuation make it difficult to understand ideas.	10
TOTAL				100

SUPPORT FOR EMERGENT BILINGUALS

When including emergent bilingual support, educators should strive to include many different multilingual texts. Most of the texts presented in the text set have several different translations available and as students look for other resources concerning their issue, they can utilize their home language to find information on how their issue has been represented in the media.

SUPPORT FOR STUDENTS WITH SPECIAL LEARNING NEEDS

Support for students with special learning needs could come in the form of providing students with extended time to complete the assignments. Students could also have the option to complete the student inquiry project in a small group or with a partner instead of working individually. Throughout the unit, students are presented with many different types of texts, from videos to infographics, which can be used to support the traditional articles that are also presented within the unit. Additionally, students are able to utilize audio functions to assist in reading articles on the computer.

SUPPORT FOR CULTURALLY RESPONSIVE EDUCATION

Educators should implement culturally responsive teaching as a form of student support. This support can come in the form of recognizing the various cultures represented in the classroom and encouraging students to utilize their home cultures in what they are learning. As students choose their issue, they may select an issue that relates to their home culture, or a culture they feel they do not know a lot about. As students look for information about how their issue is represented in the media, they can focus on their home culture and how their culture is being represented in the media.

SUGGESTED MODIFICATIONS FOR A DIFFERENT GRADE LEVEL

Students in upper elementary and middle school can benefit from a selection of topics to choose from instead of giving students the choice to choose any topic. In addition, most of the articles have leveling options, which will be good for both upper elementary and middle school students. Most videos are also appropriate for all ages; however, there are a few that may need to be replaced with videos that are better suited for upper elementary and middle school students. A great resource to find more information about historical events in U.S. history can be found at https://www.historyforkids.net/.

REFERENCES

Freire, P. (1998). *Pedagogy of freedom: Ethics, democracy, and civic courage.* Rowman & Littlefield.

Haddix, M., Garcia, A., & Price-Dennis, D. (2017). Youth, popular culture, and the media: Examining race, class, gender, sexuality, and social histories. In *Adolescent literacies: A handbook of practice-based research* (pp. 23–38). Guilford Press.

Love, B. (2019). We who are dark. In *We want to do more than survive* (pp. 1–15). Beacon Press.

Moje, E. B., Giroux, C., & Muehling, N. (2017). Navigating cultures and identities to learn literacies for life: Rethinking adolescent literacy teaching in a post-core world. In *Adolescent literacies: A handbook of practice-based research* (pp. 3–22). Guilford Press.

Reynolds, J. (2020). Can't sing and dance and write it away. In *Stamped: Racism, antiracism, and you: A remix of the national book award-winning stamped from the beginning* (pp. 147–153). Little Brown Books for Young Readers.

Wynter-Hoyte, K., & Smith, M. (2020). Hey, black child. Do you know who you are? Using African diaspora literacy to humanize blackness in early childhood education. *Journal of Literacy Research, 52*(4), 406–431. https://doi.org/10.1177/1086296X20967393

Part IV

EXPLORING THE DIVERSE LIVED EXPERIENCES OF MODERN-DAY ADOLESCENTS

Figure PIV.1 Love Is Universal. *Ema Martin.*

Many of the chapter authors in this section experienced adolescence during the 1990s and 2000s. While not too long ago, day-to-day life both in and out of school has changed drastically for young people today. Contemporary adolescents live both on- and off-line and navigate many seemingly adult issues. Adolescents' lived experiences are more than we can imagine. From reminders of American gun culture in their schools to the closeting of their true selves, we must give voice to all of their myriad identities so that they can see themselves through windows, mirrors, and sliding glass doors to a more inclusive future (Bishop, 1990).

The following section gives voice to the life-worlds of contemporary adolescents through including their identities, literacies, and lived experiences. We hope that in this section students will see themselves and their experiences valued and be able to critique history as it happens. Even more so, we hope that they will answer the call Reynolds and Kendi (2020) give their readers in *Stamped:* To choose if they would "be a segregationist (hater), an assimilationist (a coward), or an antiracist (someone who truly loves). Choice is yours. Don't freak out. Just breathe in. Inhale. Hold it. Now exhale slowly: NOW" (p. 247).

Bishop, R. S. (1990). Mirrors, windows, and sliding glass doors. *Perspectives*, 6(3), ix–xi.

Reynolds, J., & Kendi, I. X. (2020). *Stamped: Racism, antiracism, and you.* Little, Brown and Company.

Chapter 9

The Death of Childhood

Mass Shootings in the United States

Christina Thomas

Figure 9.1 Innocence Lost. *Rachel Villarreal.*

THEME AND RATIONALE

The rate of gun violence in the United States compared to other countries is astonishingly high, with gun-related homicides in this country surpassing that of each member of the Organisation for Economic Cooperation and Development (OECD), the only exception being Mexico (Jena et al., 2014). This high rate of gun violence could potentially be a fact of which adolescents and adults living in this country are not aware, and students should be educated about the topic of gun violence if they are expected to make informed decisions as they make their way through society. Indeed, as Nardi (2015) states, "education and communication are the strongest tools in the goal to restrict access to lethal means and decrease risk for mass shooting" (p. 2).

Nardi (2015) further explains that we can reduce the risk of gun violence in adolescents if we have the will to do so. That can be achieved by educating ourselves and our students about compassion, empathy, and the signs of those who may be struggling in order to find them help before a tragedy occurs. This education can begin at any age, as we must instill a sense of responsibility and understanding in the young minds of our students at a time when they are still developing into the person they will become when they enter into adult society (Rubens & Shehadeh, 2014).

Rubens and Shehadeh (2014) stated that gun violence in schools has most commonly occurred when students feel ostracized, abused, neglected, angry, and resentful, when they lack impulse control, or in those who have an affinity for guns and violent behaviors. Mass shootings and violent tragedies can be prevented by first identifying those with mental issues who may be at risk of committing a violent act (McGinty et al., 2014), and then by providing the necessary education and interventions to prevent these tragedies (Rubens & Shehadeh, 2014). Mass shootings and gun violence should not be topics that are censored in the classroom; ignorance in students will not foster any type of action or change and will only leave students vulnerable to the potential of violence in their society (Rubens & Shehadeh, 2014).

UNIT GOALS

This unit will introduce students to various literature regarding mass shootings in the United States and invite them to examine the details, victims, survivors, and family members affected by these tragedies. Using critical literacy and inquiry, students will be given opportunities for discussions about subject matter that is rarely addressed in a manner that will promote an understanding of the real impact that events such as these have on human beings.

Students will be given opportunities to reflect and express themselves through multimodal representations. It is only with awareness that there will be any possibility of change for our future. By opening a discussion about the topic of United States' mass shootings, students will not only be informed about this crisis but also have the opportunity to consider ideas for change and potential approaches to instill a greater sense of empathy and compassion in the American people.

MULTIMODAL TEXT SET

Admittedly, gun violence is a sensitive topic and can spark many emotions. As teachers curate their own text set, they should be mindful of students' maturity and past experiences with gun violence.

Books

- Ahmed, S. K. (2018). *Being the change: Lessons and strategies to teach social comprehension.* Heinemann.
- Archer, A., & Kleinman, L. (Eds.). (2019). *If I don't make it, I love you: Survivors in the aftermath of school shootings.* Skyhorse.
- Bernall, M. (2000). *She said yes.* Pocket Books.
- Cullen, D. (2010). *Columbine.* Twelve.
- Hernandez, A. (2020). *El día más oscuro de El Paso.* Self-published.
- Holley, J. (2020). *Sutherland Springs: God, guns, and hope in a Texas town.* Hachette Books.
- Klebold, S. (2017). *A mother's reckoning: Living in the aftermath of tragedy.* Crown.
- Linker, M. (2014). *Intellectual empathy: critical thinking for social justice.* University of Michigan Press.
- Lysiak, M. (2014). *Newtown: An American tragedy.* Gallery Books.
- Parker, A. (2017). *An unseen angel: A mother's story of faith, hope, and healing after Sandy Hook.* Shadow Mountain.
- Pollack, A., Eden, M., & Pollack, H. (2019). *Why Meadow died: The people and policies that created the Parkland shooter and endanger America's students.* Post Hill Press.
- Reid, W. H. (2018). *A dark night in Aurora: Inside James Holmes and the Colorado mass shootings.* Skyhorse.
- Roy, L. (2010). *No right to remain silent: What we've learned from the tragedy at Virginia Tech.* Crown.
- Schildkraut, J. (Ed.). (2018). *Mass shootings in America: Understanding the debates, causes, and responses.* ABC-CLIO.

Videos

- Sandy Hook Promise (2018, December 10). *Point of view (30 sec)* [Video]. YouTube. https://www.youtube.com/watch?v=4yukekoTCjI
- Sandy Hook Promise (2019, September 17). *Back-to-school essentials - Sandy Hook promise* [Video]. YouTube. https://www.youtube.com/watch?v=b5ykNZl9mTQ

- Syracuse.com (2016, December 6). *Sandy Hook promise: Gun violence warning signs* [Video]. YouTube. https://www.youtube.com/watch?v=9qyD7vjVfLI

News Reports

- BBC News (2016, June 15). *Orlando nightclub shooting: How the attack unfolded.* BBC News. https://www.bbc.com/news/world-us-canada-36511778
- CBS News (2019, October 3). *Las Vegas Shooting.* CBS News. https://www.cbsnews.com/feature/las-vegas-shooting/
- Ray, M. (2020, June 5). *Orlando shooting of 2016.* Encyclopedia Britannica. https://www.britannica.com/event/Orlando-shooting-of-2016
- Zambelich, A., & Hurt, A. (2016, June 26). *Three hours in Orlando: Piecing together an attack and its aftermath.* NPR. https://www.npr.org/2016/06/16/482322488/orlando-shooting-what-happened-update

Short Film

- McCormack, W. (Director), & Govier, M. (Director). (2020). *If anything happens, I love you* [Short film]. Netflix.

Article

- Isbell, L., Dixon, K., & Sanders, A. (2019). Arming teachers for school safety: Providing clarity for state policies. *Texas Education Review, 7*(2), 6–13. http://dx.doi.org/10.26153/tsw/2281

SAMPLE LESSONS

Table 9.1 provides a unit overview with some general teaching ideas. The Common Core State Standards (CCSS) that this unit addresses are shown in the table. All of the lessons below follow the mentioned standards to teach English language arts in the 11th and 12th grades.

Sample Lesson One: Warning Signs

Introduction Video and Response

Begin with *Sandy Hook Promise: Gun violence warning signs* video. Students will then take about 10 minutes to discuss how the video made them feel and what they are thinking with a partner. Students will write down a takeaway

Table 9.1 Unit Overview and General Teaching Ideas

Weeks One–Two
- Examine and discuss significant mass shooting events in U.S. history.
- Explore various forms of literature related to mass shootings, impact on victims and family members, and gun violence.

Common Core Standards	Some Related Texts
• CCSS.ELA-LITERACY.RH.11-12.9 Integrate information from diverse sources, both primary and secondary, into a coherent understanding of an idea or event, noting discrepancies among sources. • CCSS.ELA-LITERACY.RL.11-12.1 Cite strong and thorough textual evidence to support analysis of what the text says explicitly as well as inferences drawn from the text, including determining where the text leaves matters uncertain. • CCSS.ELA-LITERACY.RL.11-12.2 Determine two or more themes or central ideas of a text and analyze their development over the course of the text, including how they interact and build on one another to produce a complex account; provide an objective summary of the text.	• Video: Sandy Hook Promise: Gun violence warning signs https://www.youtube.com/watch?v=9qyD7vjVfLI • Book: *Columbine* • Book: *Sutherland Springs: God, Guns, and Hope in a Texas Town* • Book: *Newtown: An American Tragedy* • Book: *She Said Yes* • Book: *Why Meadow Died: The People and Policies That Created the Parkland Shooter and Endanger America's Students* • Book: *A Dark Night in Aurora: Inside James Holmes and the Colorado Mass Shootings* • Book: *No Right to Remain Silent: What We've Learned from the Tragedy at Virginia Tech* • Book: *Mass Shootings in America: Understanding the Debates, Causes, and Responses* • News report: Orlando nightclub shooting: How the attack unfolded https://www.bbc.com/news/world-us-canada-36511778 • New report: Las Vegas Shooting https://www.cbsnews.com/feature/las-vegas-shooting/ • News report: Orlando shooting of 2016 https://www.britannica.com/event/Orlando-shooting-of-2016 • News report: 3 hours in Orlando: Piecing together an attack and its aftermath https://www.npr.org/2016/06/16/482322488/orlando-shooting-what-happened-update

Weeks Three–Four
- Provide various classroom activities and assignments with the objective of opening discussions regarding possible avenues for change.
- Learn about research related to gun violence, responses, and explore proposals for change.
- Explore various forms of literature related to mass shootings, impact on victims and family members, and gun violence.

(Continued)

Table 9.1 Unit Overview and General Teaching Ideas (*Continued*)

Common Core Standards	Some Related Texts
• CCSS.ELA-LITERACY.RH.11-12.7 Integrate and evaluate multiple sources of information presented in diverse formats and media (e.g., visually, quantitatively, as well as in words) in order to address a question or solve a problem. • CCSS.ELA-LITERACY.RH.11-12.9 Integrate information from diverse sources, both primary and secondary, into a coherent understanding of an idea or event, noting discrepancies among sources. • CCSS.ELA-LITERACY.RL.11-12.1 Cite strong and thorough textual evidence to support analysis of what the text says explicitly as well as inferences drawn from the text, including determining where the text leaves matters uncertain. • CCSS.ELA-LITERACY.RL.11-12.2 Determine two or more themes or central ideas of a text and analyze their development over the course of the text, including how they interact and build on one another to produce a complex account; provide an objective summary of the text.	• Video: Point Of View | Sandy Hook Promise https://www.youtube.com/watch?v=4yukekoTCjl • Book: *A Mother's Reckoning: Living in the Aftermath of Tragedy*

Weeks Five–Six
- Examine and discuss significant mass shooting events in U.S. history.
- Explore various forms of literature related to mass shootings, their impact on victims and family members, and gun violence.
- Provide various classroom activities and assignments with the objective of opening discussions regarding possible avenues for change.
- Learn about research related to gun violence, responses, and explore proposals for change.
- Explore various forms of literature related to mass shootings, their impact on victims and family members, and gun violence.

(*Continued*)

Table 9.1 Unit Overview and General Teaching Ideas (*Continued*)

Common Core Standards	Some Related Texts
• CCSS.ELA-LITERACY.RH.11-12.7 Integrate and evaluate multiple sources of information presented in diverse formats and media (e.g., visually, quantitatively, as well as in words) in order to address a question or solve a problem. • CCSS.ELA-LITERACY.RH.11-12.9 Integrate information from diverse sources, both primary and secondary, into a coherent understanding of an idea or event, noting discrepancies among sources. • CCSS.ELA-LITERACY.RL.11-12.1 Cite strong and thorough textual evidence to support analysis of what the text says explicitly as well as inferences drawn from the text, including determining where the text leaves matters uncertain. • CCSS.ELA-LITERACY.RL.11-12.2 Determine two or more themes or central ideas of a text and analyze their development over the course of the text, including how they interact and build on one another to produce a complex account; provide an objective summary of the text.	• Book: *She Said Yes* • Book: *Columbine* • Book: Sutherland Springs: God, Guns, and Hope in a Texas Town • Book: A Mother's Reckoning: Living in the Aftermath of Tragedy • Book: Newtown: An American Tragedy • Book: An Unseen Angel: A Mother's Story of Faith, Hope, and Healing After Sandy Hook • Book: Why Meadow died: The People and Policies That Created the Parkland Shooter and Endanger America's Students • Book: A Dark Night in Aurora: Inside James Holmes and the Colorado Mass Shootings • Book: No Right to Remain Silent: What We've Learned from the Tragedy at Virginia Tech • Book: If I Don't Make It, I Love You: Survivors in the Aftermath of School Shootings • Book: Mass Shootings in America: Understanding the Debates, Causes, and Responses • News report: Orlando nightclub shooting: How the attack unfolded https://www.bbc.com/news/world-us-canada-36511778 • New report: Las Vegas Shooting https://www.cbsnews.com/feature/las-vegas-shooting/ • News report: Orlando shooting of 2016 https://www.britannica.com/event/Orlando-shooting-of-2016 • News report: 3 hours in Orlando: Piecing together an attack and its aftermath https://www.npr.org/2016/06/16/482322488/orlando-shooting-what-happened-update

they got from the video and write it on a sticky note to be placed in the front of the room. Discuss some of the sticky notes as a class to gain a general sense of emotions that the video evoked.

Group Reading/Research and Presentation

Students will divide themselves into groups of three to four and be assigned or choose a tragedy to research. There are several resources that can be found in the text set provided, or students may use any other research database to which they have access. Students will share their learning with classmates in any format they choose (written summary, oral presentation, multimedia presentation, song, rap, poem, etc.). The purpose is to inform their classmates about vital and impactful information regarding the tragedy they researched.

Additional Reading, Response, and Discussion

In addition to in-class reading, students will read choosing one of the books found in the text set, such as *She Said Yes*; *An Unseen Angel: A Mother's Story of Faith, Hope, and Healing After Sandy Hook*; *If I Don't Make It, I Love You: Survivors in the Aftermath of School Shootings*; *A Mother's Reckoning: Living in the Aftermath of Tragedy*; *Why Meadow Died: The People and Policies that Created the Parkland Shooter and Endanger America's Students*. They may also use any other book of their choice which addresses the impact these tragedies have on victims and their loved ones.

Students will be grouped in 3s or 4s and discuss their self-selected reading choice. Topics discussed should include key concepts, how the tragedy affected the lives of those involved, and proactive strategies for deterring tragedies like these in the future.

We will begin reading the book *Columbine* as a class and discuss as we read. Students will write response papers to each day's reading as an exit ticket.

Assessment Option

After one or two weeks, when the in-class reading of *Columbine* has concluded, students will synthesize their learning of the in-class reading and their personal reading choice. Students will create class presentations in any format of their choosing (poem, rap, essay, video, comic or graphic novel, PowerPoint, song, image collage, etc.) to discuss key points with the class about the tragedy they researched. Students will also discuss the personal impact their subject has had on them personally, as well as the impact on the community where the tragedy occurred.

Sample Lesson Two: Developing Empathy

Introduction Video, Response, and Discussion

Students will watch the *Point Of View | Sandy Hook Promise* video. Students will take about 10 minutes to discuss with a partner how the video made them feel and what they are thinking. Students will write down a takeaway they got from the video and write it on a sticky note to be placed in the front of the room. Discuss some of the sticky notes with the class.

In-Class Reading

In-class reading will be *A Mother's Reckoning: Living in the Aftermath of Tragedy* to understand that victims of the shooter are not the only ones that are impacted by these tragedies. Students will write response papers to each day's reading as an exit ticket.

When readings have concluded, the teacher will lead a class discussion with a focus on empathy and the need for interventions for students that struggle with emotional and mental issues.

Group Reading Discussion

Students will be grouped in 3s or 4s and discuss the class readings. Included in discussions will be key concepts, how the tragedy affected the lives of those involved, and proactive strategies for deterring tragedies like these in the future.

Extended Learning Option

In addition to in-class reading, students will read *She Said Yes*. Allow 15 minutes per day of class time for students to read their individual reading and/ or discuss their readings with classmates.

Assessment Option

Students will think about ways to deter tragedies like these in the future and come up with an action plan for future change and intervention. Groups will share their action plans with the class upon completion of the assignment.

GUIDELINES FOR A STUDENT INDIVIDUAL INQUIRY PROJECT

Students will choose one of the mass shootings and research a victim, survivor, friend, or family member impacted by the tragedy. The following prompts may be used:

- How have they been impacted by the tragedy?
- What is something you think they would do differently if they could?
- Imagine being in their shoes. How would you act and feel?

Students will create a product from their perspective as a tribute to this victim, survivor, friend, or family member, such as a poem, narrative, video message or tribute, song, blog, or image collage. Table 9.2 is a rubric that teachers may use to assess student learning during the inquiry project.

Table 9.2 Tribute Rubric for Student Inquiry Project

Individual Inquiry Project Rubric	Exceeded Expectations	Met Expectations	Did Not Meet Expectations
Research	Life of the victim, survivor, friend, or family member was thoroughly and thoughtfully researched. Various sources were looked into in order to gather a true understanding of this person's life and emotions, before and after the tragedy.	Life of the victim, survivor, friend, or family member was thoroughly researched. Sources were looked into in order to gather a true understanding of this person's life and emotions after the tragedy.	Life of the victim, survivor, friend, or family member was not well researched. Few sources were looked into in order to gather an understanding of this person's life.
Creative Project	The project was creative and well constructed. A substantial amount of time was spent on idea, presentation, and thoughtfulness in order to ensure the victim, friend, or family member was honored in a respectful and meaningful manner.	The project was well constructed. Time was spent on idea, presentation, and thoughtfulness in order to ensure the victim, friend, or family member was honored in a respectful manner.	The project was not well constructed. Not much time was spent on idea, presentation, and thoughtfulness. The project was not constructed in a respectful manner.

SUPPORT FOR EMERGENT BILINGUALS

Teachers can accommodate students in need of language support by using the following strategies:

- Students may watch the video *Back-To-School Essentials - Sandy Hook Promise* with Spanish subtitles at https://www.youtube.com/watch?v=96u

mLIao2Oc. Students will be given the opportunity to respond and discuss using the language they are most comfortable with.
- Students who can read in Spanish may read the book *El Día Más Oscuro de El Paso* for their reading option during class.
- Students may work with their peers to translate and discuss texts in the language of their choosing.

SUPPORT FOR STUDENTS WITH SPECIAL LEARNING NEEDS

Teachers can provide students in need of accommodations and modifications by using the following strategies:

- Allow students the option of giving oral or multimodal responses (such as artwork or graphics) rather than written responses to videos and readings.
- Students may work in small groups for their inquiry project and reading assignments and may choose to have assignments read aloud to them. Students will also have reduced reading requirements.
- Provide students the option to receive individualized, scaffolded, and explicit instruction from the teacher and/or peers.

DIFFERENT GRADE LEVEL MODIFICATIONS

Modifying this curriculum unit for younger students will require more discussion and group work, less individual reading, and project requirements. There will also be fewer research requirements, more scaffolding, prompts, and teacher-led activities as students learn how to analyze and synthesize information from multiple sources. There will be more focus on empathetic aspects of the curriculum rather than focusing so much on details of the tragedies which may be traumatizing for younger students. Taking one day to learn about gun violence in general might help students in earlier grades understand why they are participating in active shooter or lockdown drills.

REFERENCES

Jena, A. B., Sun, E. C., & Prasad, V. (2014) Perspective: Does the declining lethality of gunshot injuries mask a rising epidemic of gun violence in the United States *Journal of General Internal Medicine, 29*(7), 1065–1069.

McGinty, E. E., Webster, D. W., Jarlenski, M., & Barry, C. L. (2014). News media framing of serious mental illness and gun violence in the United States, 1997–2012. *American Journal of Public Health, 104*(3), 406–413.

Nardi, D. (2015). Decreasing risk for mass shootings in the United States. *Journal of Psychosocial Nursing and Mental Health Services, 53*(12). doi: 10.3928/02793695-20151116-22

Rubens, M., & Shehadeh, N. (2014). Gun violence in United States: In search for a solution. *Frontiers in Public Health, 2*(17). https://doi.org/10.3389/fpubh.2014.00017

Chapter 10

Rap Music

Leveraging Hip-Hop Culture to Empower

Victor Antonio Lozada

Figure 10.1 Lin-Manuel Miranda. *Angela Gonzalez.*

THEME AND RATIONALE

Our students have many different assets with which they can access the classroom curriculum, but those assets are sometimes seen as deficits because they are not a part of the majoritized culture (Babino & Stewart, 2020; Paris & Alim, 2017). One asset that many students have is an understanding and appreciation of hip-hop culture. Rap permeates hip-hop culture and helps to connect youth to their identity, politics, and language (Alim, 2011; Alim & Pennycook, 2007). Giving students the opportunity to express their assets through rap is paramount in allowing them to see themselves in school. This curriculum unit leverages the creative power of rap as a tool that gives students access to their identity, politics, and language.

Adolescence is a time period for identity development. Giving students opportunities to explore their identities through media in which they are adept at expressing opens doors to understanding their reality in new ways for life (Moje et al., 2017). Rap music provides multiple opportunities for students to see themselves reflected in the text and music. A variety of rap artists including Blacks, Asians, Whites, Latinx, and women can connect with a myriad of youth. Providing windows, mirrors, and sliding glass doors through which students see themselves allows for an easier time in connecting with their political identities (Bishop, 1990).

The politics of hip-hop culture and by extension rap rest between the intersection of race and language (Alim, 2011). The themes in rap music expose students to a variety of topics including police brutality, anti-Blackness, and urban blight among other topics. Giving students the opportunity to interact with these topics develops a critical consciousness (Freire, 2018). Upon understanding the intersection of race and language, they can use their critical consciousness to not only critique their lived experiences but also the ways in which language can be used to racialize them.

The power of language is evident in rap music. Students can use their critical consciousness to critique the ways in which the mono-mainstream culture (Babino & Stewart, 2020) oppresses their ways of life. Raciolinguistics is one aspect of this oppression (Rosa & Flores, 2020). Raciolinguistics is the conflation of "racialized bodies with linguistic deficiency unrelated to any objective linguistic practice" (Flores & Rosa, 2015, p. 150). Rap music often has a history of being seen from a deficit point of view (Ogbar, 2007; Westhoff, 2016). However, through a critical consciousness, students can begin to question the raciolinguistic ideologies present in the mono-mainstream culture that generally looks at hip-hop culture from a deficit point of view and work to show that it should not be looked at in this way but instead from an antiracist perspective (Kendi, 2019).

Bringing identity, politics, and language together through the lens of rap music allows for students to interact with English language arts, social studies, and music standards. This gives students the ability to express their full linguistic-experiential reservoirs (Rosenblatt, 1989, p. 164) while expressing themselves in a multimodal way (Beach et al., 2017; Wissman, 2017). This curriculum unit shows some of the myriad of ways that students can interact with curriculum on their own terms through rap music.

UNIT GOALS

This unit will engage all students' literacies. From engaging their critical literacies in understanding the politics inherent in rap to applying their digital literacies in creating multimodal compositions for their raps, students will identify with the content and engage with English language arts, social studies, and music standards. The goal is to help students find themselves as writers and creators within a school-based literacy in order to see the value in what they know.

This unit starts with having students find their identity through different rap artists. While an attempt was made to include as many different facets of rap, no collection of rap artists is complete. The artists suggested in lesson one are just that: suggestions. The hope is that some of your students will find artists to whom they relate.

After your students identify with rap artists, they will be guided through the ways in which politics imbues most rap. Childish Gambino's *This Is America* will be the mentor text from which students will be asked to create their own rap that reflects their lived experiences.

Lastly, your students will use their rap as a basis for a multimodal creation of expression. Students will create a presentation in a format of their choices (suggestions include video, presentation software, or live performance), which will engage not only English language arts objectives but also music objectives.

MULTIMODAL TEXT SET

Picture Books

- Giovanni, N. (2008). *Hip-hop speaks to children: A celebration of poetry with a beat.* Sourcebooks, Inc.
- Hill, L. C. (2013). *When the beat was born: DJ Kool Herc and the creation of hip hop.* Roaring Brook Press.
- Jonze, S. (2020). *Beastie boys.* Rizzoli.
- Queen Latifah. (2006). *Queen of the Scene.* HarperCollins.

Videos

- 1theK. (2015, December 24). *[MV] Yoonmirae (윤미래) _ Black Happiness (검은 행복)* [Video]. YouTube. https://www.youtube.com/watch?v=1DK-MPh7vKk
- Arcane. (2020, August 16). *The success of Drake (Drake documentary)* [Video]. YouTube. https://www.youtube.com/watch?v=uggLILO8pOY

- BeforeTheyWereFamous (2016, August 22). *Pitbull | Before They Were Famous | Biography* [Video]. YouTube. https://www.youtube.com/watch?v=ZGoGzH1j8NE
- BeforeTheyWereFamous (2019, September 6). *Post Malone | Before They Were Famous | Epic Biography From 0 to Now* [Video]. YouTube. https://www.youtube.com/watch?v=umn60LjWS2A
- DelicatelyDurable (2014, June 21). *CNN Spotlight: Pitbull (2014)* [Video]. YouTube. https://www.youtube.com/watch?v=ONdMj4-nb5M
- Empressive (2018, June 30). *Ms Lauryn Hill's Unsung Music Story: Battle with the Music Industry and Her Legacy* [Video]. YouTube. https://www.youtube.com/watch?v=g7FemWggfkk
- Genius (2018, August 27). *How 'The Miseducation of Lauryn Hill' Changed Hip-Hop | Genius News* [Video]. YouTube. https://www.youtube.com/watch?v=iiUOi0l7oE0
- Goldthread (2019, December 19). *Jony J: The Biggest Chinese Rapper You've Never Heard Of - East Coast (S1E7)* [Video]. YouTube. https://www.youtube.com/watch?v=KhXE3KwOLdk
- More Music Shows (2020, May 15). *The Beastie Boys The Story Of (2004)* [Video]. YouTube. https://www.youtube.com/watch?v=C-0fYtUCF14
- Nichebender (2020, May 16). *Snoop Dogg documentary.* [Video]. YouTube. https://www.youtube.com/watch?v=3BCLYtliy50
- Power 105.1. (2020, July 1). *Missy Elliot & Timbaland Sit With The Breakfast Club (2013)* [Video]. YouTube. https://www.youtube.com/watch?v=RQlIrfx8hrU
- RealRealityGossip (2020, April 4). *The TRUTH about Missy Elliott's life story.* [Video]. YouTube. https://www.youtube.com/watch?v=cSaiOAESf40
- RealRealityGossip (2020, June 6). *Queen Latifah's SAD life story.* [Video]. YouTube. https://www.youtube.com/watch?v=jQeGFpirP7E
- Sway's Universe (2019, August 29). *Missy talks untold industry tales, marriage, Jay Z epiphany + new music* [Video]. YouTube. https://www.youtube.com/watch?v=qJJserYphQI

Chapter Books

- Ardis, A. (2013). *Inside a thug's heart.* Kensington Books.
- Baker, S. (2018). *The history of gangsta rap: From Schooly D to Kendrick Lamar, the rise of a great American art form.* Abrams.
- Belmont and Belcourt Biographies. (2012). *Drake: An unauthorized biography.* Price World Publishing.
- Bezdecheck, B. (2009). *Missy Elliott.* Rosen Publishing.
- Bozza, A. (2019). *Not afraid: The evolution of Eminem.* Hachette Books.
- Bozza, A. (2003). *Whatever you say I am: The life and times of Eminem.* Crown Publishers.

- Bradley, A. (2017). *Book of rhymes: The poetics of hip hop.* Civitas.
- Bradley, A., & DuBois, A. (Eds.). (2010). *The anthology of rap.* Yale University Press.
- Brookshire Harris, T. (2016). *Billionaire branding: How hip hop cash kings built their empire.* Brookshire Book Group.
- Brown, R. (2014). *Pitbull.* Mitchell Lane Publishers.
- Calkhoven, L. (2018). *Lin-Manuel Miranda (You should meet).* Simon Spotlight.
- Chang, J. (2007). *Can't stop won't stop: A history of the hip-hop generation.* St. Martin's Press.
- Collins, T. B. (2012). *Missy Elliott.* Infobase Publishing.
- Cotts, N. (2009). *Hip-hop: Pitbull.* Mason Crest.
- Diamond, M., & Horovitz, A. (2018). *Beastie boys book.* Spiegel & Grau.
- Dogg, S., & Seay, D. (2000). *Tha Doggfather: The times, trials, and hardcore truths of Snoop Dogg.* HarperCollins.
- Duthel, C. (2012). *Pitbull: Mr. worldwide.* Author.
- Eminem. (2000). *Angry blonde.* HarperEntertainment.
- Eminem. (2008). *The way I am.* E. P. Dutton.
- Higgins, D. (2012). *Far from over: The music and life of Drake, the unofficial story.* ECW Press.
- Iandoli, K. (2019). *God save the queens: The essential history of women in hip-hop.* Dey Streets Books.
- Lusted, M. A. (2019). *Post Malone: Rapper, singer, and songwriter.* Abdo.
- McQuillar, T. L., & Johnson, F. L. (2010). *Tupac Shakur: The life and times of an American icon.* Hachette Books.
- Morgan, J. (2018). *She begat this: 20 years of* The Miseducation of Lauryn Hill. Atria.
- Nickson, C. (1999). *Lauryn Hill: She's got that thing.* St. Martin's.
- Parker, S. F. (Ed.). (2014). *Eminem and rap, poetry, race: Essays.* McFarland.
- Queen Latifah. (1998). *Ladies first: Revelations of a strong woman.* William Morrow.
- Queen Latifah. (2010). *Put on your crown: Life-changing moments on the path to queendom.* Grand Central Publishing.
- Reese, E. (2018). *The history of hip hop.* Barnes and Noble Press.
- Reynolds, S. (2011). *Bring the noise: 20 years of writing about hip rock and hip hop.* Soft Skull Press.
- Saddleback Educational Publishing. (2013). *Pitbull (Hip-hop biographies).* Author.
- Schwartz, H. E. (2019). *Lin-Manuel Miranda: Revolutionary playwright, composer, and actor.* Lerner Publications.
- Shakur, T. (1999). *The rose that grew from concrete.* MTV Books.
- Thomas, A. (2019). *On the come up.* HarperCollins.
- Zwickel, J. (2011). *Beastie boys: A musical biography.* ABC-CLIO.

Informational Articles

- Biography.com Editors (2021, January 19). *Drake - Songs, families, and facts - Biography*. Biography. https://www.biography.com/musician/drake
- DT MFBTY International (2015, April 9). *[Interview] Yoonmirae opens up about her background, MFBTY, and the current Korean hip-hop scene.* https://drunkentigerintl.com/2015/04/09/news-yoon-mirae-opens-up-about-her-background-mfbty-and-the-current-korean-hip-hop-scene/
- Editors of *Encyclopaedia Britannica* (2021, March 14). *Queen Latifah: American musician and actress.* Britannica. https://www.britannica.com/biography/Queen-Latifah
- Jony J. (2021). In *Baidu*. https://baike.baidu.com/item/Jony%20J
- Maylkm. (2021, March 7). *Details about Yoon Mi-rae's songs that transcend genres.* https://www.moinnet.com/en/unfamiliar-koreans/t-yoon-mi-rae/
- Smith, D. (2019, January 11). Hamilton in Puerto Rico: A joyful homecoming...but it's complicated. *Guardian*. https://www.theguardian.com/stage/2019/jan/11/hamilton-musical-puerto-rico-joyful-homecoming-but-complicated
- Touré. (2003, October 30). The mystery of Lauryn Hill. *Rolling Stone*. https://www.rollingstone.com/music/music-news/the-mystery-of-lauryn-hill-249020/
- Weiner, J. (2017, November 17). Post Malone: Confessions of a hip-hop rock star. *Rolling Stone*. https://www.rollingstone.com/music/music-features/post-malone-confessions-of-a-hip-hop-rock-star-116218/
- Zhou, Z. (2019, August 8). *Who is Jony J and how did J. Cole inspire him to become China's "hip-hop-poet"?* https://www.goldthread2.com/identity/jony-j-rap-china/article/3021935

Podcasts

- Chace, Z. (Host). (2010, June 28). The many voices of Lauryn Hill. In *All Things Considered*. NPR. https://www.npr.org/2010/06/28/128149135/the-many-voices-of-lauryn-hill
- Nelson, D., & Silva, N. (Producers). (2018, September 6). Keepers of the underground: The hiphop archive at Harvard. In *Morning Edition*. WBUR. https://www.npr.org/2018/09/06/641599819/keepers-of-the-underground-the-hiphop-archive-at-harvard
- Pearson, V., & Martin, R. (Hosts). (2018, October 29). Rap, Buddhism and broken radiators: The Beastie Boys have a story for everything. In *Morning Edition*. WBUR. https://www.npr.org/2018/10/29/661647527/rap-buddhism-and-broken-radiators-the-beastie-boys-have-a-story-for-everything

SAMPLE LESSONS

The sample lessons in this section come from the general teaching ideas and standards in Table 10.1. Teachers may use other teaching ideas in this book as well as other texts they locate about this topic to develop various lesson plans to guide student learning.

Sample Lesson One: Identity (Inquiry Project)

Objective: Students will be able to research a rap icon to whom they relate and create a multimodal presentation of that rap artist.
Learning Target: I can research a rap artist. I can develop a multimodal presentation to show the rap artist's life and music.
Materials:
- Multimodal Text Set including highlighted rappers.
- Computer with software such as Google Slides, Prezi, or PowerPoint.

Procedure:
1. Independent reading of rap artists (examples listed below from Multimodal Text Set)
   a. Black rappers
      i. Tupac Shakur
      ii. Drake
      iii. Snoop Dogg
   b. Asian rappers
      i. Yoon Mi-rae (Tasha)
      ii. Jony J
      iii. MC Jin
   c. Latinx rappers
      i. Lin-Manuel Miranda
      ii. Pitbull
   d. White rappers
      i. Eminem
      ii. Beastie Boys
      iii. Post Malone
   e. Female rappers
      i. Lauryn Hill
      ii. Queen Latifah
      iii. Missy Elliott
2. Small-group discussion about their rap artists.
3. Students prepare an individual presentation using software such as Google Slides, Prezi, or PowerPoint based on what they read and what they talked about concerning their rap artist.

Table 10.1 Unit Overview and General Teaching Ideas

Week One: Identity through Rap
- Inquiry Project—Rap Icon
  - Identity through rap icons
  - Research of rap icons

Common Core Standards	Some Related Texts
• CCSS.ELA-Literacy.W.11-12.6 Use technology, including the internet, to produce, publish, and update individual or shared writing products in response to ongoing feedback, including new arguments or information. • CCSS.ELA-Literacy.W.11-12.7 Conduct short as well as more sustained research projects to answer a question (including a self-generated question) or solve a problem; narrow or broaden the inquiry when appropriate; synthesize multiple sources on the subject, demonstrating understanding of the subject under investigation. • CCSS.ELA-Literacy.W.11-12.8 Gather relevant information from multiple authoritative print and digital sources, using advanced searches effectively; assess the strengths and limitations of each source in terms of the task, purpose, and audience; integrate information into the text selectively to maintain the flow of ideas, avoiding plagiarism and overreliance on any one source and following a standard format for citation. • CCSS.ELA-Literacy.RH.11-12.1 Cite specific textual evidence to support analysis of primary and secondary sources, connecting insights gained from specific details to an understanding of the text as a whole.	Tupac Shakur • *The Rose that Grew from Concrete* by Tupac Shakur • *Inside a Thug's Heart* by Angela Ardis Drake • *Far from Over: The Music and Life of Drake* by Dalton Higgins • *Drake: An Unauthorized Biography* by Belmont and Belcourt Biographies Snoop Dogg • *The Doggfather: The Times, Trials, and Hardcore Truths of Snoop Dogg.* by Snoop Dogg and David Seay Yoon Mi-rae • Yoon Mi-rae, Black Happiness https://www.youtube.com/watch?v=1DK-MPh7vKk • Details behind Yoon Mi-rae's songs that transcend genres https://www.moinnet.com/en/unfamiliar-koreans/t-yoon-mi-rae/ Jony J • Jony J: The Biggest Chinese Rapper You've Never Heard Of https://www.youtube.com/watch?v=KhXE3kwOLdk • Jony J https://baike.baidu.com/item/Jony%20J (Available in Chinese or English via Google Translate)

- CCSS.ELA-Literacy.RH.11-12.2
Determine the central ideas or information of a primary or secondary source; provide an accurate summary that makes clear the relationships among the key details and ideas.

MC Jin
- Not Just an "Asian Rapper": MC Jin Talks Identity, Politics, and China Behind New Standup Special https://radiichina.com/mc-jin-identity-politics-standup-special/
- Jin Au Yeung: The Story https://www.youtube.com/watch?v=_qlAEh-5x_U

Lin-Manuel Miranda
- *Guardian* article "Hamilton in Puerto Rico: A joyful homecoming...but it's complicated" (ADAPTATION - article available in Spanish and at a variety of reading levels via Newsela) https://www.theguardian.com/stage/2019/jan/11/hamilton-musical-puerto-rico-joyful-homecoming-but-complicated
- *Lin-Manuel Miranda (You Should Meet)* by Laurie Calkhoven and Alyssa Petersen

Pitbull
- *Hip-hop: Pitbull* by Nat Cotts
- *Pitbull: Hip-hop Biographies* by Saddleback Educational Publishing

Eminem
- *The Way I Am* by Eminem
- *Not Afraid: The Evolution of Eminem* by Anthony Bozza

Beastie Boys
- *Beastie Boys Book* by Michael Diamond and Adam Horovitz
- *Beastie Boys* by Spike Jonze, Mike Diamond, and Adam Horovitz

Post Malone
- Before They Were Famous: Post Malone https://www.youtube.com/watch?v=umn60LjWS2A
- *Post Malone: Rapper, Singer, and Songwriter* by Marcia Amidon Lusted

(Continued)

Table 10.1 Unit Overview and General Teaching Ideas (*Continued*)

	Lauryn Hill • *She Begat This: 20 Years: 20 Years of the Miseducation of Lauryn Hill* by Joan Morgan https://www.rollingstone.com/music/music-news/the-mystery-of-lauryn-hill-249020/ • *The Mystery of Lauryn Hill* https://www.rollingstone.com/music/music-news/the-mystery-of-lauryn-hill-249020/ Queen Latifah • *Ladies First: Revelations of a Strong Woman* by Queen Latifah • *Queen of the Scene* by Queen Latifah and Frank Morrison Missy Elliott *Missy Elliott* by Bethany Bezdecheck The TRUTH about Missy Elliott's Life Story https://youtu.be/cSaiOAESf40

Week Two: Politics through Rap

- Rap Analysis
  - Childish Gambino's *This Is America*
- Rap Writing
  - Textual references
  - Politics and political identity

Common Core Standards	Some Related Texts
• CCSS.ELA-Literacy.RL.11-12.1 Cite strong and thorough textual evidence to support analysis of what the text says explicitly as well as inferences drawn from the text, including determining where the text leaves matters uncertain. • CCSS.ELA-Literacy.RL.11-12.2 Determine two or more themes or central ideas of a text and analyze their development over the course of the text, including how they interact and build on one another to produce a complex account; provide an objective summary of the text.	• Chapter 25 from *Stamped* by Jason Reynolds and Ibram X. Kendi • Childish Gambino *This Is America* https://youtu.be/VYOjWnS4cMY • *Washington Post* article "This Is America": Breaking down Childish Gambino's powerful new music video https://www.washingtonpost.com/news/arts-and-entertainment/wp/2018/05/07/this-is-america-breaking-down-childish-gambinos-powerful-new-music-video/

- CCSS.ELA-Literacy.RL.11-12.3

  Analyze the impact of the author's choices regarding how to develop and relate elements of a story or drama (e.g., where a story is set, how the action is ordered, how the characters are introduced and developed).

- CCSS.ELA-Literacy.RL.11-12.4

  Determine the meaning of words and phrases as they are used in the text, including figurative and connotative meanings; analyze the impact of specific word choices on meaning and tone, including words with multiple meanings or language that is particularly fresh, engaging, or beautiful. (Include Shakespeare as well as other authors.)

- CCSS.ELA-Literacy.RL.11-12.6

  Analyze a case in which grasping a point of view requires distinguishing what is directly stated in a text from what is really meant (e.g., satire, sarcasm, irony, or understatement).

- CCSS.ELA-Literacy.RL.11-12.7

  Analyze multiple interpretations of a story, drama, or poem (e.g., recorded or live production of a play or recorded novel or poetry), evaluating how each version interprets the source text. (Include at least one play by Shakespeare and one play by an American dramatist.)

- ADAPTATIONS—Newsela version of the *Washington Post* article, video version from the *Washington Post* article (subtitled) https://www.youtube.com/watch?v=qfqVkEYQ1Ls
- *Book of rhymes: The poetics of hip hop* by Adam Bradley

Week Three: Language through Rap

Common Core Standards	Some Related Texts
- CCSS.ELA-Literacy.W.11-12.6 Use technology, including the internet, to produce, publish, and update individual or shared writing products in response to ongoing feedback, including new arguments or information.	- Student-created rap text from the previous week. - Childish Gambino *This Is America* https://youtu.be/VYOjWnS4cMY

Assessment/Evaluation Artifact: Student-created multimodal report on a rap artist.

Sample Lesson Two: Politics and Rap

Objective: The student will be able to analyze multiple interpretations of Childish Gambino's *This Is America* and create a rap (poem) in this style using the writing process.

Learning Target: I can analyze Childish Gambino's *This Is America* from multiple points of view. I can write a rap to discuss political issues.

Materials:
- Chapter 25 from *Stamped* by Jason Reynolds and Ibram X. Kendi
- Childish Gambino *This Is America* https://youtu.be/VYOjWnS4cMY
- *Washington Post* article "This Is America": Breaking down Childish Gambino's powerful new music video. https://www.washingtonpost.com/news/arts-and-entertainment/wp/2018/05/07/this-is-america-breaking-down-childish-gambinos-powerful-new-music-video/
- Adaptions—Newsela version of the article, video version from the *Washington Post* article (subtitled) https://www.youtube.com/watch?v=qfqVkEYQ1Ls

Procedures:
1. Independent reading of Chapter 25 from *Stamped*.
2. Whole group—Watch Childish Gambino's *This Is America*.
3. Whole-group discussion—What themes were in the music video?
4. Independent reading—*Washington Post* article (adaptations for developing readers available through Newsela and YouTube video from *Washington Post*).
5. Small Group—Discuss how the *Washington Post* article may have changed your point of view and what topics interest you.
6. Independent Work—Create a rap that illuminates a social issue like *This Is America*.

Assessment/Evaluation Artifact: Students create a rap (poem) that illuminates a social issues of their choice. Figure 10.2 is a 5th grade student's poem about historical treatment of migrant farm workers during the time Dolores Huerta co-founded the National Farmworkers Association with Cesar Chavez. This illustrates how rap connects to poetry and how younger adolescents could engage with this unit.

Sample Lesson Three: Language

Objectives: The student will create a multimodal presentation of their rap.

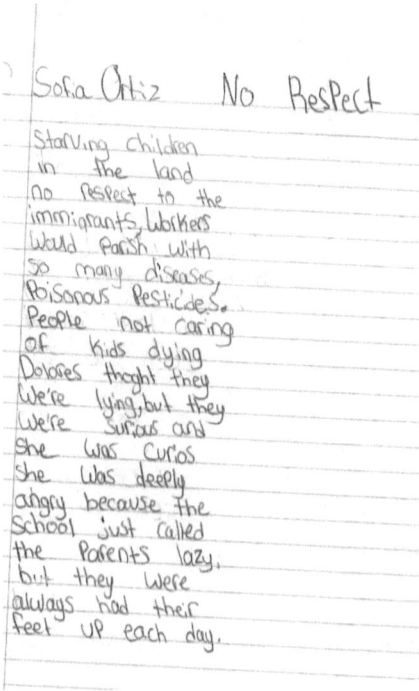

Figure 10.2 No Respect. *Sofia Ortiz.*

Learning Target: I can create a multimodal presentation of my rap.
Materials:
- Computer with internet capabilities
- Software possibilities—Music Creation
- https://www.musicca.com/drum-machine
- Audacity
- Garageband

Software possibilities—Multimodal Presentation
- PowerPoint
- Google Slides
- Prezi

Procedure:
1. Whole-group instruction on using online sampling and digital presentations: Choose one or two applications that your students have access to and that they might already have used for another project. Explain how they will use this application to create their own rap text set to music.
2. Individual work investigating three rap videos as mentor texts (examples in Multimodal Text Set such as *This Is America* or *Happiness is*

Black): Provide students structure during this individual work time by guiding them in what to notice from the videos. Have them take notes or complete a graphic organizer about the following elements of the (school-appropriate) rap videos they choose to watch and analyze:
- Sounds: How would you describe the beat? What does it suggest?
- Words: What message does the spoken word convey?
- Images: What images are included in the video? How do they contribute to the overall message the artist/s wanted to convey?

3. Individual work creating a multimodal presentation with rap text set to music.
4. Small group work discussing creations.
5. Individual work revising work as per the comments of their peers.
6. Whole-group presentation.

Assessment/Evaluation Artifact: Multimodal digital presentation of the student's rap (poem). Table 10.2 is a rubric to assess student learning for their rap set to music.

SUPPORT FOR EMERGENT BILINGUALS

- Numerous texts are available in Spanish, Chinese, and Korean. Google translate can be leveraged to understand websites in a variety of languages (translate.google.com).
- Nonlinguistic adaptations such as those offered through music are also available.
- Students should be encouraged to use their full linguistic repertoire and produce texts in that way.

SUPPORT FOR STUDENTS WITH SPECIAL LEARNING NEEDS

- Numerous texts are audio- or video-based to provide for multiple avenues of understanding the information.
- Closed-captioning for videos on YouTube for students with auditory processing disorders or hearing impairments is available.
- Use the text for podcasts for students with auditory processing disorders or hearing impairments.
- Students can access a variety of reading levels offered through Newsela.

Table 10.2 Rap Text Rubric

	Outstanding (4)	Proficient (3)	Developing (2)	Emerging (1)
Artifact	The artifact is created in a way that conveys the author's meaning *and* shows a deep understanding of the medium.	The artifact is created in a way that *sometimes* conveys the author's meaning *and sometimes* shows a deep understanding of the medium.	The artifact is created in a way that *sometimes* conveys the author's meaning *or sometimes* shows a deep understanding of the medium.	The artifact is created in a way that *may* convey the author's meaning *or may* show a deep understanding of the medium.
Context (Rhetorical Skills)	The artifact shows deep regard for the social context in which it will be.	The artifact *often* shows deep regard for the social context in which it will be.	The artifact *sometimes* shows deep regard for the social context in which it will be.	The artifact *may* show deep regard for the social context in which it will be.
Substance	The artifact deals with the subject matter in a deep way.	The artifact *often* deals with the subject matter in a deep way.	The artifact *sometimes* deals with the subject matter in a deep way.	The artifact *may* deal with the subject matter in a deep way.
Process Management and Technical Skills	The student can *always* show evidence of editing.	The student can *often* show evidence of editing.	The student can *sometimes* show evidence of editing.	The student *may* show evidence of editing.
Habits of Mind	The student can *always* show evidence of the use of Habits of Mind.	The student can *often* show evidence of the use of Habits of Mind.	The student can *sometimes* show evidence of Habits of Mind.	The student *may* show evidence of Habits of Mind.

Note: There are many different conceptions of Habits of Mind. Wahleithner (2014) referenced the *Framework for Success in Postsecondary Writing*, which includes curiosity, openness, engagement, creativity, persistence, responsibility, flexibility, and metacognition (Council of Writing Program Administrators et al., 2011).

DIFFERENT GRADE LEVEL MODIFICATIONS

- Lesson 2 might be adapted for younger adolescents by using a different song. Instead of using Childish Gambino's *This Is America*, the teacher might try using Erykah Badu's *Master Teacher* along with Lozada's (2020) explanation of artistic citizenship to see how students can use music in a way to express their reality.

REFERENCES

Alim, H. S. (2011). Global ill-literacies: Hip hop cultures, youth identities, and the politics of literacy. *Review of Research in Education, 35*(1), 120–146. https://doi.org/10.3102/0091732X10383208

Alim, H. S., & Pennycook, A. (2007). Glocal linguistic flows: Hip-hop culture(s), identities, and the politics of language education. *Journal of Language, Identity & Education, 6*(2), 89–100. https://doi.org/10.1080/15348450701341238

Babino, A., & Stewart, M. A. (2020). *Radicalizing literacies and languaging: A framework toward dismantling the mono-mainstream assumption*. Palgrave Macmillan.

Beach, R., Castek, J., & Scott, J. (2017). Acquiring processes for responding to and creating multimodal digital productions. In K. A. Hinchman & D. A. Appleman, (Eds.), *Adolescent literacies: A handbook of practice-based research*, (pp. 292–309). The Guilford Press.

Bishop, R. S. (1990). Mirrors, windows, and sliding glass doors. *Perspectives, 6*(3), ix–xi.

Common Core State Standards Initiative. (2020). English language arts standards. http://www.corestandards.org/ELA-Literacy/

Council of Writing Program Administrators, National Council of Teachers of English, & National Writing Project. (2011). *Framework for success in postsecondary writing*. Creative Commons.

Flores, N., & Rosa, J. (2015). Undoing appropriateness: Raciolinguistic ideologies and language diversity in education. *Harvard Educational Review, 85*(2), 149–171. https://doi.org/10.17763/0017-8055.85.2.149

Freire, P. (2018). *Pedagogy of the oppressed (50th anniversary edition)*. Bloomsbury Academic.

Kendi, I. X. (2019). *How to be an antiracist*. One World.

Lozada, V. (2020). Music to make a positive difference. *The Orff Echo, 53*(1), 51–54.

Moje, E. B., Giroux, C., & Muehling, N. (2017). Navigating cultures and identities to learn literacies for life: Rethinking adolescent literacy teaching in a post-core world. In K. A. Hinchman & D. A. Appleman, (Eds.), *Adolescent literacies: A handbook of practice-based research* (pp. 3–20). The Guilford Press.

Ogbar, J. O. G. (2007). *Hip-hop revolution: The culture and politics of rap*. University Press of Kansas.

Paris, D., & Alim, H. S. (2017). *Culturally sustaining pedagogies: Teaching and learning for justice in a changing world.* Teachers College Press.

Rosa, J., & Flores, N. (2020). Reimagining race and language: From raciolinguistic ideologies to a raciolinguistic perspective. In H. S. Alim, A. Reyes, & P. V. Kroskrity (Eds.), *The Oxford Handbook of Language and Race* (pp. 90–107). Oxford University Press.

Rosenblatt, L. M. (1989). Writing and reading: The transactional theory. In J. M. Mason (Ed.), *Reading and writing connections* (pp. 153–176). Allyn & Bacon.

Wahleithner, J. M. (2014). The National Writing Project's Multimodal Assessment Project: Development of a framework for thinking about multimodal composing. *Computers and Compositions, 31*, 79–86. http://doi.org/10.1016/j.compcom.2013.12.004

Westhoff, B. (2016). *Original Ganstas: The untold story of Dr. Dre, Easy-E, Ice Cube, Tupac Shakur, and the birth of West Coast rap.* Hachette Books.

Wissman, K. (2017). "No more paperwork!" Student perspectives on multimodal composition in response to literature. In K. A. Hinchman & D. A. Appleman, (Eds.), *Adolescent literacies: A handbook of practice-based research* (pp. 257–275). Guilford Press.

Chapter 11

Consent Isn't Complicated
The Implications of the #MeToo Movement
Christina Thomas

Figure 11.1 Untitled, Me Too. *Paige Walter.*

THEME AND RATIONALE

Sexual harassment and sexual violence inside and outside of the workplace is something that far too many women, as well as men, have experienced (Airey, 2018). According to Jagsi (2018), over 50 percent of women living in the United States have been a victim of this type of sexual misconduct during their lifetime. Unfortunately, many people in today's society have become far too comfortable with this fact, even to the point that survivors have become accustomed to blaming themselves when they become a victim of sexual harassment and sexual violence (Bond, 2017).

Sexual harassment is so prevalent that it is often used for comedic effect in Hollywood TV and films, predominately in the past, where audience members would not so much as give it a second thought and accept the occurrence as a humorous joke (Halgas, 2006). "It is the little things woven into our social structures that contribute to and maintain systematic oppression" (Bond, 2017, p. 214).

The #MeToo movement has played a hugely successful part in "defamiliarizing" these common occurrences by shining light on survivors and their stories (Airey, 2018). By introducing this movement into school curricula, students will also be made aware of these incidences and understand that they should not be tolerated or accepted as normalized behavior, thus creating space and inspiration for change (Moore & Begoray, 2017).

Sexual harassment may begin at a young age (Marie Claire, 2018), and by introducing the #MeToo movement to students they will be able to see that they too have a voice and there are a variety of ways they will be able to use that voice to launch and propel a conversation to encourage learning, strength, and change for themselves as well as for our society (Moore & Begoray, 2017). The #MeToo movement is a powerful avenue for approaching the issue of sexual harassment in the classroom, which will, in turn, allow students the opportunities to question toxic public, work, and home environments. Then, they can become activists for justice, tolerance, and equity to change the status quo (Bond, 2017).

UNIT GOALS

Students will learn about and discuss the #MeToo movement and the impact it has had on our society, specifically in regard to its impact on survivors of sexual harassment and sexual violence. Students will understand the history of this movement, learn about the founder of the movement, be introduced to multimodal texts which demonstrate varying perspectives on the topic of sexual harassment and sexual violence, and develop their own thoughts and ideas about how to create a safer society for men and women alike.

MULTIMODAL TEXT SET

Books

- Anderson, L. H. (2011). *Speak*. Square Fish.
- Bradley, K. B. (2020). *Fighting Words*. Dial Books.
- Brian, R. (2020). *Consent (for kids!): Boundaries, respect, and being in charge of you*. Little, Brown and Company.
- Dershowitz, A. (2019). *Guilt by accusation: The challenge of proving innocence in the age of #MeToo*. Hot Books.
- Gieseler, C. (2019). *The voices of #MeToo: From grassroots activism to a viral roar*. Rowman & Littlefield Publishers.
- Greene, M. (2018). *The little #MeToo book for men*. ThinkPlay Partners.
- Guest Pryal, K. R. (2019). *Even if you're broken: Essays on sexual assault and #MeToo*. Blue Crow Books.
- Ito, S. (2021). *Black xox: The memoir that sparked Japan's #MeToo movement* (A. M. Powell, Trans.). The Feminist Press at CUNY.
- Kantor, J., & Twohey, M. (2020). *She said: Breaking the sexual harassment story that helped ignite a movement*. Penguin Books.
- Kurtzman-Counter, S. (2014). *Miles is the boss of his body*. The Mother Company.
- Russell, K. E. (2020). *My dark Vanessa: A novel*. William Morrow.
- Siegel, S. (2020). *Fractured*. Shay Siegel.
- Smith, A. (2017). *The way I used to be*. Margaret K. McElderry Books.

Videos

- Marie Claire. (2018, February 6). *Growing up in the #MeToo movement* [Video]. YouTube. https://www.youtube.com/watch?v=Y3Wkb74TEtA
- Me Too Movement (2018, April 10). *This is the 'me too.' movement* [Video]. YouTube. https://www.youtube.com/watch?v=ZF55ItXWjck&t=2s
- Me Too Movement (2020, October 15). *'Me too.' Act too* [Video]. YouTube. https://www.youtube.com/watch?v=1SuC0iVNjnQ
- Rob Bliss Creative (2014, October 28). *10 hours of walking in NYC as a woman* [Video]. YouTube. https://www.youtube.com/watch?v=b1XGPvbWn0A
- TED (2019, January 4). *Me Too is a movement, not a moment - Tarana Burke* [Video]. YouTube. https://www.youtube.com/watch?v=zP3LaAYzA3Q

Graphic Novel

- Una. (2016). *Becoming unbecoming*. Arsenal Pulp Press.

Websites

- me too (2021). *me too: Research and literature.* https://metoomvmt.org/learn-more/research-literature/
- me too (2021). *me too: Statistics.* https://metoomvmt.org/learn-more/statistics/
- me too (2021). *me too: Take action.* https://metoomvmt.org/take-action/
- me too (2021). *me too: You are not alone.* https://metoomvmt.org/

News Reports

- Pflum, M. (2018, October 15). *A year ago, Alyssa Milano started a conversation about #MeToo. These women replied.* NBC News. https://www.nbcnews.com/news/us-news/year-ago-alyssa-milano-started-conversation-about-metoo-these-women-n920246

YouTube Channel

- Me Too Movement (n.d.) *Home* [YouTube channel]. YouTube. https://www.youtube.com/c/MeTooMovementOfficial/featured

Social Media

- Milano, A. [@Alyssa_Milano]. (2017, October 15). *If you've been sexually harassed or assaulted write 'me too' as a reply to this tweet.* Twitter. https://twitter.com/alyssa_milano/status/919659438700670976?lang=en

Article

- Alexander, K. L. (2020). *Tarana Burke.* National Women's History Museum. https://www.womenshistory.org/education-resources/biographies/tarana-burke

Film

- Cohen, B. (Director), Shenk, J. (Director), Berge, R. (Producer), & Dosa, S. (Producer). (2016). *Audrie and Daisy* [Film]. Actual Films; Netflix.

SAMPLE LESSONS

General teaching ideas, as well as Common Core State Standards (CCSS), are shown in Table 11.1. The sample lessons draw from the contents in the table.

Table 11.1 Unit Overview and General Teaching Ideas

Week One
- Explore a text set related to the #MeToo movement, sexual harassment, and sexual violence issues.
- Students will explore varying perspectives on sexual harassment and sexual violence in order to build empathy for survivors' varying experiences.

Common Core Standards	Some Related Texts
• CCSS.ELA-LITERACY.RH.11-12.7 Integrate and evaluate multiple sources of information presented in diverse formats and media (e.g., visually, quantitatively, as well as in words) in order to address a question or solve a problem. • CCSS.ELA-LITERACY.RH.11-12.9 Integrate information from diverse sources, both primary and secondary, into a coherent understanding of an idea or event, noting discrepancies among sources. • CCSS.ELA-LITERACY.RL.11-12.2 Determine two or more themes or central ideas of a text and analyze their development over the course of the text, including how they interact and build on one another to produce a complex account; provide an objective summary of the text.	• Video: This Is the "me too." Movement: https://www.youtube.com/watch?v=ZF55ItXWjck&t=2s • Book: *Speak* • Book: *Fractured* • Book: *Becoming Unbecoming* • Book: *The Way I Used to Be* • Book: *Fighting Words* • Video: Me Too Movement: https://www.youtube.com/c/MeTooMovementOfficial/featured • Website: Statistics: https://metoomvmt.org/learn-more/statistics/ • Website: https://metoomvmt.org/

Week Two
- Students will read and learn about how this movement began, its founder, Tarana Burke, and its impact on society.
- Students will learn statistics on sexual harassment and sexual violence and be made aware of how common these occurrences can be.
- Students will explore diverse perspectives on sexual harassment and sexual violence in order to build empathy for survivors' varying experiences.

Common Core Standards	Some Related Texts
• CCSS.ELA-LITERACY.RH.11-12.7 Integrate and evaluate multiple sources of information presented in diverse formats and media (e.g., visually, quantitatively, as well as in words) in order to address a question or solve a problem. • CCSS.ELA-LITERACY.RH.11-12.9 Integrate information from diverse sources, both primary and secondary, into a coherent understanding of an idea or event, noting discrepancies among sources.	• Video: 10 Hours of Walking in NYC as a Woman: https://www.youtube.com/watch?v=b1XGPvbWn0A • Book: *She Said: Breaking the Sexual Harassment Story That Helped Ignite a Movement* • Video: Growing Up in the #MeToo Movement: https://www.youtube.com/watch?v=Y3Wkb74TEtA

(Continued)

Table 11.1 Unit Overview and General Teaching Ideas (*Continued*)

Common Core Standards	Some Related Texts
• CCSS.ELA-LITERACY.RL.11-12.1 Cite strong and thorough textual evidence to support analysis of what the text says explicitly as well as inferences drawn from the text, including determining where the text leaves matters uncertain. • CCSS.ELA-LITERACY.RL.11-12.2 Determine two or more themes or central ideas of a text and analyze their development over the course of the text, including how they interact and build on one another to produce a complex account; provide an objective summary of the text.	• Video: "me too." Act Too: https://www.youtube.com/watch?v=1SuC0iVNjnQ&feature=emb_logo • Article: Tarana Burke: https://www.womenshistory.org/education-resources/biographies/tarana-burke • Video: Me Too is a movement, not a moment | Tarana Burke: https://www.youtube.com/watch?v=zP3LaAYzA3Q • Video: Growing Up in the #MeToo Movement: https://www.youtube.com/watch?v=Y3Wkb74TEtA • Film: *Audrie and Daisy*

Week Three
- Students will review everything they have learned about the #MeToo movement.
- Students will engage in discussions regarding possible avenues for change.
- Students will brainstorm and put into action their ideas to make a difference in a way they believe will make a difference in the #MeToo movement.

Common Core Standards	Some Related Texts
• CCSS.ELA-LITERACY.RH.11-12.7 Integrate and evaluate multiple sources of information presented in diverse formats and media (e.g., visually, quantitatively, as well as in words) in order to address a question or solve a problem. • CCSS.ELA-LITERACY.RH.11-12.9 Integrate information from diverse sources, both primary and secondary, into a coherent understanding of an idea or event, noting discrepancies among sources.	• Video: "me too." Act Too: https://www.youtube.com/watch?v=1SuC0iVNjnQ&feature=emb_logo • Website: Take Action: https://metoomvmt.org/take-action/ • Website: Take Action: Advocate Toolkit: https://metoomvmt.org/take-action/action-toolkits/

Sample Lesson One: Unit Introduction

This lesson is designed to cover multiple class periods. Teachers may include any number of texts students view or read, depending on the amount of time they have available to them. Multiple weeks may be needed in order for students to complete the YA novel they choose.

Introduction Video, Group Discussion, and Personal Response

Students will watch *This Is the "Me Too" Movement* as an introduction to the unit. After watching the video, allow time for small group discussions where students will share their knowledge on the movement and how they feel about the impact it has had on our society. Provide each student with their own personal journal to begin writing down their thoughts and reactions throughout this unit, as some aspects may be incredibly personal for them. These journals do not need to be collected or reviewed by the teacher.

Multimodal Research, Reflection, and Discussion

Students will spend time watching videos from the *Me Too Movement* YouTube channel as an exercise to build empathy for survivors of sexual harassment and sexual violence. Students may do so in partners or individually, and will spend time discussing the videos with each other and reflecting in their journals.

Allow time for self-selected reading. After the allotted time for exploration, discussion, and written reflections of the videos, have students select one of the articles from the text set to read. After reading, they respond in their journal and share their learning with a partner.

Representation of Knowledge

Students will write a summary of one of the survivors' videos they've watched or read about. They may also create an essay, poem, or any other multimodal representation created from the perspective of a sexual harassment survivor they've learned about. Included in their assignment should be personal and important information shared by the survivor, new information they've learned about the #MeToo movement and sexual harassment, and/or any information that they feel may be important for their classmates to know. Their finished product will be presented to the class and/or displayed in the classroom for students to read and reflect on when time permits. The teacher may use this product as an assessment of student learning.

Ongoing Self-Selected Reading and Reflections

Students will choose the young adult novel they would like to read during the duration of this unit. Students will spend time researching and deciding which book they would be interested in reading. Students will choose from the books *Speak, Fractured, Becoming Unbecoming, The Way I Used to Be, Fighting Words*, or any other book they may feel is relevant or impactful for them.

Students will be allowed 15 minutes per class to read their self-selected novel, and 10 minutes per class to write reflections in their personal journals. If they are reading the same novel as others in the class, the teacher may also allow time for literature response group discussion.

Extended Learning Options

Students will spend time outside of class reviewing statistics from https://metoomvmt.org/. Students will come to the class prepared to share one statistic they found shocking or impactful.

When students have completed their self-selected reading assignments, they will create presentations for their classmates to view. The presentation can be in any multimodal format of their choosing (comic strips, video, essay, rap, song, illustration, graphics, poem, PowerPoint, images, etc.). The presentation can be about any aspect of the book that they would like to discuss, including a summary, personal impact, relevant information about sexual harassment and sexual violence, warning signs to be aware of, etc. Presentations can be completed in groups of students who read the same book or students who read different books who would like to compare and contrast, or individually.

Sample Lesson Two: Reflecting and Taking Action

Introduction

Students will begin class by watching *10 Hours of Walking in NYC as a Woman*.

Discussion

The class will discuss the unwanted attention this woman had to endure and how this video can raise awareness about the kind of harassment that many women and men may experience.

Reflection

Students will watch *Growing Up in the #MeToo Movement* to view and understand perspectives from young girls. Ask students to write a reflection based on the two videos using the following guiding questions:

- Have you ever experienced (or known anyone who experienced) any of the situations described in the videos?
- Have you ever felt disrespected just because of who you are? If so, how did that make you feel?

Students will not write their names on the reflections. If they choose to do so, students will post their reflections up in the classroom so other students may read them. (Make sure this is voluntary.) This is an exercise to build empathy and awareness among students. Figure 11.2 illustrates one student's reflection that she chose to share.

Closure

Students will watch *"me too: Act Too"* as the class begins thinking about what kind of action they can take in order to make a difference.

Students will brainstorm innovative ways to educate others about sexual harassment and sexual violence, similar to the way the *10 Hours of Walking in NYC as a Woman* video demonstrated sexual harassment from this woman's experience. How will students "Act Too" in order to raise awareness? Students will analyze and synthesize their learning from the literature and videos they've experienced in order to identify what aspects have been the most impactful for them and which aspects could potentially be just as inspiring to others.

Sample Lesson Three: Founding the Movement

Introduction

Students will begin learning all about Tarana Burke, the founder of the #MeToo movement. Ask them if they have heard her name in any of their previous reading or viewing and what they have learned about her.

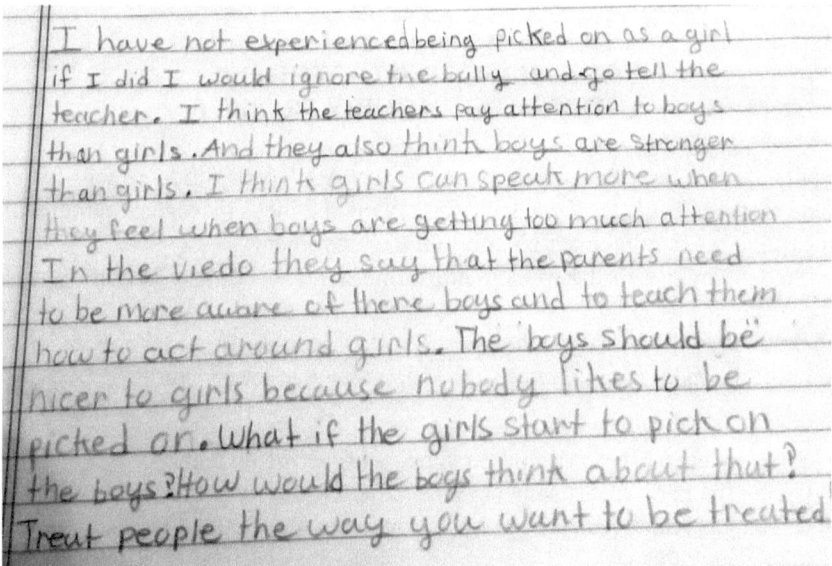

Figure 11.2   Student Work. *Catherine Thomas.*

Reading/Viewing

Students will read the biography referenced in the text set, *Tarana Burke*, and watch her TED talk, *Me Too is a movement, not a moment | Tarana Burke*, in order to learn about and understand the person she is and her beliefs.

Reflection

Students will write a reflection about who Tarana Burke is as a person and why the work she is doing is so important. Allow students to get into small groups or partners to discuss their reflections with each other.

Extended Learning Options

Students will begin reading *She Said: Breaking the Sexual Harassment Story That Helped Ignite a Movement* in class to gain insight into one of the more publicized aspects of the #MeToo movement.

Students can watch the film *Audrie and Daisy* during their free time if they choose to, as this film may not be suitable for all students. Students who choose not to watch the film can search social media and Twitter threads for more #MeToo posts and statements. They can come to the class prepared to share during whole group and small group discussions about how they chose to extend their knowledge and what they've learned from their experience and/or their reflections.

GUIDELINES FOR A STUDENT INDIVIDUAL INQUIRY PROJECT

Students will be given the opportunity to "Act Too." Students will watch *"me too: Act Too" Act Too* again and review the ideas they've come up with regarding ways to take action and join the movement.

Students will visit the website https://metoomvmt.org/take-action/ for further ideas.

Students will decide on the approach they would like to take in order to support the movement. Options for action they can take include:

- Write letters to Tarana Burke in support of the movement.
- Create flyers or advertisements promoting awareness of the movement.
- Create a research report or presentation in any multimodal format intended to educate others.
- Summarize key objectives in the *Take Action: Advocate Toolkit* (located in the text set and on the Me Too Movement website).

- Donate to the movement.
- Use social media platforms, podcasts, or blogs to raise awareness.

Students are not limited to these options and may choose any idea they may devise.

Assessment

Assessment of student performance will be based on student effort, thoughtfulness, effectiveness, and creativity related to their choice of contribution (see Table 11.2.)

SUPPORT FOR EMERGENT BILINGUALS

Support for emergent bilinguals can be provided to students using the following strategies:

- Students may work with their peers to translate and discuss texts in the language of their choosing.
- Students will be given the option to submit assignments, assessments, and presentations in the language of their choosing.

Table 11.2 Act Too Inquiry Project Rubric

Individual Inquiry Project Rubric	Exceeded Expectations	Met Expectations	Did Not Meet Expectations
Research	Various sources were used in order to gather information and ideas related to the Me Too movement and what sort of contribution could be made.	Some sources were used in order to gather information about the Me Too movement.	Few sources were used in order to gather information and explore avenues of contribution.
Creative Project	The project was creative and well constructed. A substantial amount of time was spent on idea, presentation, and thoughtfulness.	The project was well constructed. Time was spent on idea, presentation, and thoughtfulness.	The project was not well constructed. Not much time was spent on idea, presentation, and thoughtfulness.

- Students will be allowed the use of multimodal literacies (visuals, audio recordings, videos, etc.) for research, assignments, assessments, and presentations.
- Students may gain special insight into global perspectives by researching the #MeToo movement or similar initiatives in other countries by using their language skills. Spanish speakers can investigate the influential #NiUnaMas campaign in Mexico and research feminicide or *feminicidio*.

SUPPORT FOR STUDENTS WITH SPECIAL LEARNING NEEDS

Assistance can be provided for students in need of accommodations and modifications using the following strategies:

- Students may be given the opportunity for individual discussions with the teacher in regard to sensitive topics.
- Students will be provided with the option to represent their learning in any manner they choose and will be allowed the opportunity to demonstrate learning in small-group or one-on-one settings.
- Students may work in small groups for their inquiry project and reading assignments and may receive assistance from the teacher to research and develop a plan for action.

DIFFERENT GRADE LEVEL MODIFICATIONS

Younger students can begin this curriculum unit with the *Growing Up in the #MeToo Movement* video and discuss or write a reflection on their response to this video. More emphasis in the unit will be placed on boundaries, respect, empathy, and personal space. There should be fewer research and individualized reading assignments, increased scaffolding and teacher-led discussions for younger grades. Students should understand what the Me Too movement is and why it is important; however, they should not be provided with graphic or traumatizing details regarding survivors' sexual harassment and sexual violence stories.

REFERENCES

Airey, J. L. (2018). #MeToo. *Tulsa Studies in Women's Literature, 37*(1), 7–13. https://doi.org/10.1353/tsw.2018.0000

Bond, C. E. (2017). Catcalling and the college classroom: A model for teaching students about street harassment. *Feminist Teacher, 27*(2–3), 211–232. https://doi.org/10.5406/femteacher.27.2-3.0211

Halgas, J. T. L. (2006). Don't try this at home: Using a multilayered approach to teach the law of sexual harassment and sexual harassment investigations. *The Journal of Legal Studies Education, 23*(2), 217–241. https://doi.org/10.1111/j.1744-1722.2006.00029.x

Jagsi, R., & Phil, D. (2018). Sexual harassment in medicine - #MeToo. *The New England Journal of Medicine, 378*(3), 209–211. http://dx.doi.org/10.1056/NEJMp1715962

Marie Claire. (2018, February 6). *Growing up in the #MeToo movement* [Video]. YouTube. https://www.youtube.com/watch?v=Y3Wkb74TEtA

Moore, A., & Begoray, D. (2017). "The last block of ice": Trauma literature in the high school classroom. *Journal of Adolescent & Adult Literacy, 61*(2), 173–181. https://doi.org/10.1002/jaal.674

Chapter 12

See Us

LGBTQ+ Issues for Representation, Empathy, and Justice

Christina Salazar

Figure 12.1 **Equality for All.** *Zuri Emore.*

THEME AND RATIONALE

In American society, and by extension in American schools, homosexuality and gender nonconformity are often deemed inappropriate. The expectation is that individuals should closet themselves, not mention their families or relationships, so as to keep others from discomfort. Queer people exist. They are in your classroom every year. Their children and families are in your classroom every year. There is nothing controversial about their existence.

There are individuals in our country who do not agree with homosexuality, as though they have been granted the stamp of approval that all citizens are subject to. Sometimes this rejection of the homosexual and gender nonconformist is insidiously veiled as trying to keep sexual content away from children. There is no more sexual content in discussing a homosexual relationship than in discussing a heterosexual relationship. There is no more sexuality in discussing a homosexual family than in discussing a heterosexual relationship. Flores (2016) implemented an LGBTQ+ (lesbian, gay, bisexual, transgender, queer [or sometimes questioning], and others) multicultural literature unit in an elementary school classroom. He found, through this research study, that the topic of sex did not arise. Children discussed topics of adoption, civil rights, and family. The most common theme to emerge was that of acceptance of differences (Flores, 2016). Through this unit of study, students will not be discussing sex, of course, but they will study civil rights and human rights.

All people of the LQBTQ+ community deserve dignity, respect, and acknowledgment. They should not have to hide or pretend in our classrooms. This unit on LGBTQ+ issues is a unit of study of civil rights and people who deserve to be heard. Well-meaning educators often self-censor to avoid an imagined conflict. These conflicts may arise, and they should. Heteronormativity is a dangerous assumption, which underscores much of our society. It is the assumption that heterosexual attraction is normal, natural, and ideal (Thompson, 2014). Heteronormativity is dangerous in that it falsely presents one narrative as "just the way things are" and pushes out and marginalizes people, our students, who do not fit with that narrative. This exclusion and closetting of queer children is a real and measurable danger to those children.

Silence is complicity. It is an abuse of privilege and power to decide to omit homosexual narratives for one's own convenience and comfort. School can be an unsafe place for LGBTQ+ students and educators have a responsibility to address that issue. Approximately twice as many lesbian, gay, or bisexual students are bullied on school campuses than heterosexual students (Kann et al., 2018). That inequity magnifies when considering cyberbullying. Ten percent of LGBTQ+ students are missing school for fear of their own safety (Kann et al., 2018). Educators must change the narratives on their campuses to make schools a safe and welcoming environment for all students. The bullying LGBTQ+ youth endure has real effects. Homosexual and bisexual youth are five times more likely to attempt suicide than heterosexual youth (CDC, 2016). This unit of study will serve to use the curriculum for an exploration of LGTBA+ rights and experience. This work centers on the experiences of queer youth, validating them while creating empathy and understanding in heterosexual and gender-conforming students. We have the power to change the lives of our LGBTQ+ students. We have the power and the responsibility to empower them.

UNIT GOALS

Through this unit of study, students will engage with and explore issues related to LGBTQ+ rights and experiences. The goal of the unit is to empower queer students and develop empathy in heterosexual and gender-conforming students. While this curriculum unit is designed around 11th grade students, modifications for application to other grades are included. Each day of study focuses on a different aspect of LGBTQ+ existence, acknowledging that, while many issues overlap, there are differences in experience and injustice.

MULTIMODAL TEXT SET

The following section contains a list of resources which are used in this unit of study and which can be used to extend or modify the unit to fit the needs and interests of different classrooms. Educators should not feel limited by the structures laid out in the provided lessons. The framework was provided for convenience, but each teacher is an expert in their classroom. These resources could be used to spark classroom discussion, to introduce or close a lesson, or to provide additional resources for students who are working ahead of schedule or who would like to explore the issues further. The novels and long-form nonfiction selections are highly recommended. A good implementation of longer texts could be in small-group novel studies or book clubs.

Articles

- Associated Press (2020). Justices rule LGBT people protected from job discrimination. *Newsela.com*.
- History.com (2017). How did the rainbow flag become an LGBT symbol? *Newsela.com*.
- *The Guardian* (2019). LGBT people of color refuse to be erased after Orlando. *Newsela.com*.
- *Washington Post* (2019). Racial divide in the LGBT community. *Newsela.com*.

Teacher Resources/More Lessons

- American Library Association (2021). Stonewall Book Awards. https://www.ala.org/rt/rrt/award/stonewall
- Southern Poverty Law Center. (2021). Gender & Sexual Identity. https://www.learningforjustice.org/topics/gender-sexual-identity
- Mr. Vacca. (2020). Guide to Google Sites in 2020 - Create your own free website with ease! [Video]. YouTube. https://www.youtube.com/watch?v=n-0O2ZOIpZA
- The Trevor Project. (2021). Lifeguard Workshop. https://www.thetrevorproject.org/education/lifeguard-workshop/

Videos

- Degamo, J. M. (2020, July 10). Barbie girl challenge tik tok compilation:Trans edition [Video]. YouTube. https://www.youtube.com/watch?v=jrnqOr5Krh0
- HiHo Kids. (2019, January 31). Kids meet a gay conversion therapy survivor [Video]. YouTube. https://www.youtube.com/watch?v=4q-fCuy7B40
- Seventeen. (2017, August 17). Things LGBTQ+ people wish their parents knew [Video]. YouTube. https://www.youtube.com/watch?v=_OyLRnefkgM
- TED. (2016, December 7). The urgency of intersectionality: Kimberlé Crenshaw [Video]. YouTube. https://youtu.be/akOe5-UsQ2o
- UN Human Rights. (2017, March 2). UN free & equal: The lesson [Video]. YouTube. https://www.youtube.com/watch?v=iMwvdz2Yvl0

Images

- Highsmith, C. (2012). Gay Pride Parade, San Francisco, California [Photograph]. *Library of Congress.* http://hdl.loc.gov/loc.pnp/highsm.21341
- Intersectionality [Photograph]. (n.d.). *PBS.* https://bit.ly/3thTnLT
- Knox and Jorgensen after being denied a marriage license, April 1959 [Photograph]. (1959). *Wikipedia.* https://en.wikipedia.org/wiki/Christine_Jorgensen#/media/File:Howard_Knox_and_Christine_Jorgenson.jpg
- Lane, B. (1977). Lesbian rights on the agenda at the International Women's Year conf. in Houston, Texas [Photograph]. *Library of Congress.* https://www.loc.gov/pictures/item/2013650070/
- Leffler, W. (1976). Gay rights demonstration at the Democratic National Convention, New York City. *Library of Congress* [Photograph]. http://hdl.loc.gov/loc.pnp/ppmsca.09729
- Lesbian Herstory Educational Foundation. (1980). Lesbian Herstory archives, Lesbian Herstory Educational Foundation, Inc.: In memory of the

voices we have lost [Photograph]. *Library of Congress*. http://hdl.loc.gov/loc.pnp/yan.1a38479
- Seymour, M. (1954). Christine Jorgensen 1954 [Photograph]. *Wikipedia*. https://en.wikipedia.org/wiki/Christine_Jorgensen#/media/File:Christine_Jorgensen_1954.jpg
- The Ladder, October 1957 [Photograph]. (1957). *Wikipedia*. https://en.wikipedia.org/wiki/Lesbian#/media/File:The_Ladder,_October_1957.jpg

Reference Materials

- From Britannica: (This requires a subscription so ask you school librarian for access details or alternative options.)
  - Family (2021). In *Encyclopædia Britannica*. https://school.eb.com/levels/middle/article/family/274262#277174.toc
  - Gay rights movement (2021). In *Encyclopædia Britannica*. https://school.eb.com/levels/middle/article/gay-rights-movement/324384#
  - Stonewall riots (2021). In *Encyclopædia Britannica*. https://school.eb.com/levels/middle/article/Stonewall-riots/313707
  - Transgender (2021). In *Encyclopædia Britannica*. https://school.eb.com/levels/middle/article/transgender/631118

Websites

- It Gets Better Project. (2020). It Gets Better. https://itgetsbetter.org/
- National Center for Lesbian Rights. (n.d.). Mission & history. https://www.nclrights.org/about-us/mission-history/
- National Center for Lesbian Rights. (n.d.). Born Perfect. https://www.nclrights.org/our-work/born-perfect/
- Southern Poverty Law Center. (2021). Only One Me. https://www.learningforjustice.org/classroom-resources/texts/only-one-me

Picture Books

- Austrian, J. J. (2016). *Worm loves worm*. Balzer + Bray.
- Baker Schiffer, M. (2015). *Stella brings the family*. Chronicle Books.
- Cheng Thom, K. (2017). *From the stars in the sky to the fish in the sea*. Arsenal Pulp Press.
- Genhart, M. (2019). *Rainbow: A first book of pride*. Magination Press.
- Lukoff, K. (2019). *When Aidan became a brother*. Lee & Low Books.
- Phi, B. (2019). *My footprints*. Capstone Editions.
- Sanders, R. (2018). *Pride: The story of Harvey Milk and the rainbow flag*. Random House Books for Young Readers.

- Sanders, R. (2019). *Stonewall: A building. an uprising. a revolution.* Random House Books for Young Readers.
- Thorn, T. (2019). *It feels good to be yourself: A book about gender identity.* Henry Holt and Co.
- Zolotow, C. (1972). *William's doll.* Harper & Row.

Chapter Books/Nonfiction Chapter Books

- Atta, D. (2020). *The Black flamingo.* Balzer + Bray.
- Bigelow, L. J. (2019). *Drum roll, please.* HarperCollins
- Emezi, A. (2021). *Pet.* Knopf Books for Young Readers.
- Herring Blake, A. (2020). *The mighty heart of Sunny St. James.* Little, Brown Books for Young Readers.
- Pancholy, M. (2020). *The best at it.* Balzer + Bray.
- Peck. R. (2017). *The best man.* Puffin Books
- Pitman, G. E. (2019). *Stonewall riots: Coming out in the streets.* Harry N. Abrams.
- Nazemian, A. (2019). *Like a love story.* Balzer + Bray.

SAMPLE LESSONS

Teachers may spend anywhere from a few days to two to three weeks on each of the topics presented in Table 12.1. Several effective strategies to teach these ideas are included in the sample lessons. The lessons are provided for convenience, but instructors should not feel limited to these lessons, activities, or strategies. The lessons may take several class periods, depending on students' needs and school schedules. Each teacher is an expert in their classroom and school.

It is important that teachers use this unit to support LGBTQ+ students and promote allyship. Any additional lessons should focus on individuals or rights. No student (or teacher) has the right to invalidate another's lived experience. As discussed in the rationale for this chapter, our LGBTQ+ students are among the most vulnerable in our schools and lessons and activities should never be posted as a debate. Care to establish norms and expectations prior to these lessons is vital. Some norms might include:

- We are not going to laugh or tease people about who they are.
- You have a right to your beliefs as far as they do not harm or hurt others.
- You will be respectful and mature because we are talking about people's real lives.
- Outing other people or making guesses about others' sexuality is prohibited and will be dealt with severely.

Table 12.1 Unit Overview and General Teaching Ideas

Topic One: Lesbian and Gay Rights
- Harvey Milk
- Rainbow flag
- National Center for Lesbian Rights
- Gay conversion therapy

Common Core Standards	Related Texts
• CCSS.ELA-LITERACY.RH.11-12.2 Determine the central ideas or information of a primary or secondary source; provide an accurate summary that makes clear the relationships among the key details and ideas. • CCSS.ELA-LITERACY.RH.11-12.7 Integrate and evaluate multiple sources of information presented in diverse formats and media (e.g., visually, quantitatively, as well as in words) in order to address a question or solve a problem. • CCSS.ELA-LITERACY.RH.11-12.9 Integrate information from diverse sources, both primary and secondary, into a coherent understanding of an idea or event, noting discrepancies among sources.	• *Harvey Milk and the Rainbow Flag* • Image: "The Ladder" • Webpage: National Center for Lesbian Rights—About Us • Video: "Kids meet a gay conversion therapy survivor" • Webpage: National Center for Lesbian Rights—Born Perfect

Topic Two: Intersectionality
- Group identity
- Intersectionality

Common Core Standards	Related Texts
• CCSS.ELA-LITERACY.RH.11-12.2 Determine the central ideas or information of a primary or secondary source; provide an accurate summary that makes clear the relationships among the key details and ideas. • CCSS.ELA-LITERACY.RH.11-12.7 Integrate and evaluate multiple sources of information presented in diverse formats and media (e.g., visually, quantitatively, as well as in words) in order to address a question or solve a problem. • CCSS.ELA-LITERACY.RH.11-12.9 Integrate information from diverse sources, both primary and secondary, into a coherent understanding of an idea or event, noting discrepancies among sources.	• Image: "Intersectionality" • Video: "The urgency of intersectionality"

Topic Three: Gender and Identity
- Gender
- Identity
- Art as resistance
- Inquiry Project

(*Continued*)

Table 12.1 Unit Overview and General Teaching Ideas (Continued)

Common Core Standards	Related Texts
• CCSS.ELA-LITERACY.RH.11-12.2 Determine the central idea or information of a primary or secondary source; provide an accurate summary that makes clear the relationships among the key details and ideas. • CCSS.ELA-LITERACY.RH.11-12.7 Integrate and evaluate multiple sources of information presented in diverse formats and media (e.g., visually, quantitatively, as well as in words) in order to address a question or solve a problem. • CCSS.ELA-LITERACY.RH.11-12.9 Integrate information from diverse sources, both primary and secondary, into a coherent understanding of an idea or event, noting discrepancies among sources.	• *"It feels good to be yourself: A book about gender identity"* • Reference Article: Transgender • Video: "Barbie girl challenge tik tok compilation trans edition" • Poem: "Only One Me"

Sample Lesson One: Introduction to LGBTQ+ Rights

In this lesson, students will be introduced to the history of the LGBTQ+ movement and the rainbow flag. Students will also learn to create a Google Site. This skill, outside of real-world relevance, will support the final inquiry project. An effective "how-to" video for Google Sites is provided in the "Teacher Resources" section of the multimodal text set.

Hook: Draw a Flag to Represent Yourself.

Students will briefly make an identity flag. These flags should not be copies of other flags. Students should be encouraged to choose symbols that represent themselves. The teacher can make a flag and display it as an example.

Talk: Why Did You Choose the Symbols on Your Flag? Turn and Talk.

Turn and talk is a strategy where students discuss a prompt with a preselected individual. Like all strategies, this must be taught. Therefore, if this strategy has not been used before in the classroom, explicit instructions on choosing a partner, norms, and expectations should be provided before the activity. During this strategy, the teacher circulates, further developing conversations and providing positive reinforcement.

Read: Pride: The Story of Harvey Milk and the Rainbow Flag.

The teacher will read this picture book to the class in such a way that students can see the illustrations. It is not recommended to have students read the text on their own for the sake of time, focus, and enjoyment. Students may take notes because the information in the book will be used to create a product at the end of the class.

Talk: Why Are Flags Important to People and Groups? Why Is the Rainbow Flag Important to LGBTQ+ People?

Students will need to write an informal written response before discussions can begin. Give students plenty of time to think and encourage a range of ideas. After students have written down talking points, they should turn and talk. The teacher walks around the classroom during student writing and conversation to keep conversations focused on the prompt and to provide positive reinforcement.

Write: What Can You Tell Me about Harvey Milk?

Students answer the prompt in written form to recall and synthesize learning from the book and thinking from the conversations. The teacher might choose to provide sentence stems for additional support. (Examples sentence stems are: Harvey Milk was_____. He was important because _____. The rainbow flag is _____. The rainbow flag symbolizes _____. The rainbow flag is significant because _____.) The purpose of this writing piece is to create knowledge and therefore students should use whatever language skills serve them. This might look like writing in a variety of languages and dialects and/or using images. Students with traditionally marginalized language practices, like speakers of Black English or Spanish, may benefit from specific reinforcement of the value of their thinking and language. The teacher could restate the student's thinking, praise it, and extend/ask follow-up questions.

Multimodal Application: Students Create a Google Site about Harvey Milk

The teacher provides brief instruction on the creation of a Google Site. An instructional video is included in the "Teacher Resources" section of the multimodal text set. These sites can be unpolished and should not be published, unless the student insists. The goal here is for students to spend plenty of time exploring Google Sites and building skills in order to apply those skills in the final inquiry project.

Sample Lesson Two: Continued Discussion of LGBTQ+ Rights and Issues

Students continue their learning about the LGBTQ+ rights movement and focus on the specific issue of gay conversion therapy. At the end of the lesson, students independently learn about one individual's story and create a picture book about that individual. The picture book is another product option for the final inquiry project.

Respond: Notice, Wonder, Think

The teacher projects or distributes the image "The Ladder" (from the multimodal text list). This image is the first cover from *The Ladder*, a lesbian issues magazine. Students respond to the prompts: What things do you notice about this image? What do you wonder about this image? What things does this image represent? Students can respond through discussion software, like Padlet, or use any other response method the teacher prefers, as long as thinking is valued above form. That is to say, this is not the time for a formal, Standard English, response.

Direct Instruction: National Center for Lesbian Rights

The teacher shows students the National Center for Lesbian Rights—About Us webpage (in the multimodal text set) and provides direct instruction on the history of the organization. The teacher will navigate to the "Born Perfect" section of the webpage and provide students with a brief description of the mission of Born Perfect.

Video: Kids Meet a Gay Conversion Therapy Survivor

The class watches the video of an interview with a survivor of gay conversion therapy. The video is provided in the multimodal text set.

Research: Share Someone's Story

The teacher provides students with the link to the National Center for Lesbian Rights—Born Perfect webpage (in the multimodal text set). Students will pick an individual's story and take notes on the graphic organizer in Figure 12.2. (This organizer may be useful to provide structures to help students successfully complete all independent note-taking from reading and viewing in any of the chapters.)

Multimodal Application: Create a Picture Book

In this application piece, students will create a picture book to share the information they learned about the gay conversion therapy survivor they chose. The teacher should remind students that a picture book should have two to three sentences per page, simplified language, and many pictures.

Your Name: _____	Subject: _____
Notes	**Comments/Thoughts**

Figure 12.2 Example of student note page.

Sample Lesson 3: Intersectionality

The concept of intersectionality is a vital one for all justice initiatives. There is a history of rights groups and activists ignoring the intersectionality of members in their organizations and in society. In this lesson we will still explore different aspects of their identity and begin to consider the ways those identities intersect and interact.

Talk: What Groups Do I Belong To? How Is My Life Easier or More Difficult Based on Those Different Groups? (LearningforJustice, n.d.)

For this prompt, students should jot down as many identities or groups as they can. Consider creating a competition for who can identify the most groups. The teacher may share several of their identities as examples and a starting point. Some groups/identities I belong to are: mother, wife, woman, Latinx, immigrant, White presenting, teacher, student, sister, dancer, reader, etc.

Respond: Notice, Wonder, Think.

The teacher distributes or presents the image "Intersectionality" (from the multimodal text list). Students respond to the prompts: What things do you notice about this image? What do you wonder about this image? What things does this image represent? Students can respond on paper, a discussion software, or any other response method the teacher prefers.

Direct Instruction: Intersectionality

The teacher explains the purpose for studying intersectionality during the LGBTQ+ unit, because the LGBTQ+ experience is not the same for everyone. Gender makes the experience different. Race makes the experience different. Class makes the experience different. The teacher explains to students that different identities (the groups students listed earlier) intersect and interact with each other.

Watch: Ted Talk

The class now watches the video "The urgency of intersectionality" (from the multimodal text set). Students should take notes on the provided graphic organizer or other note taking format with which they may be more familiar. The video is long. The teacher can determine, for their class, whether the video should be paused throughout for discussion or support taking notes.

Talk: What Was Something You Wrote Down That You Felt Was Important? What Were Your Thoughts about That Point?

The purpose of this discussion piece is to have students consider their main takeaway from the video and their reactions and connections. Students can respond to a partner, on paper, or in a discussion software format.

Analysis: Mind Map

Students will now go back to the analysis of their different identities. They should add more identities now. They will create a mind map of their identities and represent the way these identities interact and intersect. The teacher should demonstrate the way this looks with the identities they shared earlier.

Multimodal Application: Social Media Video

Students share their identity webs by recording a short video in the format of their preferred social media application. These absolutely do not need to be published but the video should be downloaded to their device to share with the instructor. Students may need to write a script or talking points before recording.

Sample Lesson Four: Gender Identity and Trans Rights

In this final lesson before the inquiry project, students will understand that gender is a construct that evolves and varies between cultures. Students jigsaw a reference article to learn about trans issues. Finally, students will collaboratively analyze a poem about identity.

Read: It Feels Good to be Yourself: A Book about Gender Identity

The teacher reads *It Feels Good to Be Yourself: A Book About Gender Identity* (from the multimodal text set) aloud to students. Even older students can benefit from the modeling of comprehension skills during a read-aloud. Some sentence stems for thinking aloud are: I see the author chose the word/phrase _____. The image chosen for this page shows me that _____.

Direct Instruction: Gender

The teacher provides direct instruction on gender: a society's rules about what is masculine and what is feminine. These change over time and vary across cultures. Not only have the gender roles varied over time and by culture, but there are several instances of cultures having more than two genders.

Talk: What Are Some Gender Roles That You Can Think of for Your Gender?

Students may need to be reminded that these gender rules are not concrete and this is not a time for commenting on others' adherence to these roles or discussion on the validity of these roles. It may be prudent, in some cases, for this response to be conducted through an anonymous discussion software.

Jigsaw: Reference Article

Jigsaw is an instructional strategy where each member of a group becomes an expert on a particular segment of a text. They then share their learning with their group. Groups will jigsaw the reference article "Transgender" (from the multimodal text set). Break students into groups of five each. These groups are their home groups. Number students in their home groups from 1 to 5. Students separate according to their numbers. For example, all the "Number 1s" from the home groups get together. Each number group is given ⅕ if the Transgender Encyclopedia Article (from the text set, under reference articles) to learn about. Students should be directed to write down one to five facts to take back to their homegroup. Students rejoin their home groups and everyone shares their learning.

Direct Instruction: Art and Media as Empowerment and Connection

The teacher provides context for the following part of the lesson, the video, and the poetry, by talking about how many marginalized groups find ways to express themselves, connect, and empower themselves through art and social media. Depending on students' needs, the teacher may need to explain the term "marginalized."

Watch: Tik Tok Compilation

The class watches the video "Barbie girl challenge tik tok compilation trans edition," from the multimodal text set.

Write: What Kind of Accounts Do You Follow on Social Media? Do These Accounts Relate to the Identity Maps We Made? If Not, Maybe We Could Update the Maps.

Here, students will connect the video they watched to their own lives through this prompt. They will also begin to see their time on social media as connected to their identity.

Analysis: "Only One Me"

For this poetry analysis, the teacher should prepare the next activity by cutting the poem, "Only One Me" (in the multimodal text set) into its thirty-two lines and putting one or two lines on each desk. Ideally every student will have one piece of text taped to their desk. In classes larger than thirty-two, students may have to share. There should also be a blank paper taped to the desk for student responses. Allow each student three minutes to read the lines at their desks and respond on their paper, then they move on to the next desk. Students respond by commenting on word choice, meaning, connections, or elaborating on a peer's response. The teacher should push students to elaborate on the "why" of their responses.

Exit Ticket: Connection

When there are approximately 7 minutes left in class, the teacher reads the full poem to the students. Students connect the poem to their learning about transgender issues on a post-it. Students can stick the post-its in a dedicated spot on their way out of the classroom.

Table 12.2 Rubric for Student Inquiry Project

Criteria	Details	Points
Norms	• Spelling • Grammar • Neatness • Punctuality	20
Research	• Use of reliable sources. • Completeness of information (no significant gaps in time frames, regions, etc.) • Citations	35
Presentation of Findings/Ideas	• Clarity of presentation • Thoroughness (no significant gaps between information gathered and findings). • Synthesis of information (new conclusions/thoughts drawn from information). • Ideas for remedies and solutions.	45

GUIDELINES FOR A STUDENT INDIVIDUAL INQUIRY PROJECT

The purpose of this inquiry project is to deepen students' knowledge and empathy concerning LGBTQ+ rights. Students will select an LGBTQ+ activist to research. Students should be allowed about half an hour to browse various activists and choose one they would like to explore in more depth. Consider working with your school librarian to use the resources available on your campus. The teacher may wish to provide a list for students to browse through and make their selection. A list for browsing is provided in the "Teacher Resources" section of the multimodal text set. Students take notes of their activists on a graphic organizer. If using the provided graphic organizer, students should complete the graphic organizer two or more times, five notes will not be sufficient for a project of this scale. Students may choose their presentation option: video recording, making a book, making a website, and so on. Table 12.2 illustrates a rubric to evaluate the final project.

SUPPORT FOR EMERGENT BILINGUALS AND STUDENTS WITH SPECIAL LEARNING NEEDS

The sample lessons were designed with the knowledge that students will enter a classroom with a wide variety of skills. Therefore, several modifications and accommodations to support the range of students were embedded in those lessons. The teacher is encouraged to adapt effective modifications to other lessons. A reminder of some specific accommodations follows:

- Option to research and respond in first language.
  - Encourage students to apply all of their language skills to learning. The online encyclopedias recommended in this chapter have Spanish language versions that will support research for Spanish speakers.
- Peer support.
  - When students work in groups or with partners, they can bring individual talents and support each other.
- Translation software.
  - Students should be encouraged to use translation software, like Google Translate, to access any information they need or support to understand. Google Translate can also support the educator in evaluating responses that are submitted in other languages.
- Audio of readings.
  - The suggested reference articles include the option to read the text to students. The teacher can make additional audio recordings of specific texts, like the individual's stories on the NCLR Born Perfect page, in order to increase accessibility.
- Sentence stems for writing portions.
  - Specific sentence stems are provided in the sample lessons. Depending on the needs of a particular class, the teacher may choose to provide additional sentence stems, even in "Talk" portions of the lessons.
- Multimodal options for the final project.
  - The final inquiry project has a variety of presentation options. These options give students the choice and the opportunity to work and create knowledge in the way they are most comfortable and competent. Each of the lessons ended with a multimodal application piece in order to support students in choosing their ideal presentation method for the final inquiry project. Some options for the final project include, but are not limited to: creating a picture book, creating a website, and creating a social media post.
- Curation of research by a school librarian.
  - A certified librarian can help the teacher find appropriate texts at varying reading levels so that all students have access to information.

TEACHING A MODIFIED UNIT FOR ELEMENTARY

Modify the unit to introduce elementary-aged students to issues of LGBTQ+ rights and identity. Begin by reading a portion of a reference article about LGBTQ+ rights. Britannica Elementary has one titled "Gay Rights Movement." The teacher determines the length of the portion based on the age of students. For very young children, PebbleGo has an article about same-sex parents. The teacher then shows pictures of rainbow flags and tells students

Figure 12.3 Student Work. *Natalia Salazar.*

the significance of the flag to LGBTQ+ individuals and the LGBTQ+ rights movement. This would be an excellent time to connect to lessons on flags and symbols students may have already participated in. Then read "Rainbow: A First Book of Pride" to students. Finally, students will make their own flags, including symbols which are important to them. The teacher should make a sample flag ahead of the lesson. Figures 12.3 and 12.4 illustrate examples of younger students' flags and responses to age-appropriate texts.

Figure 12.4 Student Work. *Alma Salazar.*

REFERENCES

CDC. (2016). Sexual identity, sex of sexual contacts, and health-risk behaviors among students in grades 9–12: Youth risk behavior surveillance. *Department of Health and Human Services.*

Flores, G. (2016). Best not forget lesbian, gay, bisexual, and transgender themed children's literature: A teacher's reflections of a more inclusive multicultural education and literature program. *American Journal of Sexuality Education, 11(1),* 1–17.

Kann, L., McManus, T., Harris, W. A., Shanklin, S. L., Flint, K. H., Queen, B., & Ethier, K. A. (2018). Youth risk behavior surveillance—United States, 2017. MMWR. *Surveillance Summaries, 67(8),* 1–114.

Thompson, S. (2014). *Encyclopedia of Diversity and Social Justice.* Rowman & Littlefield.

Afterword

CREATE COLLECTIVE MAGIC

The years 2020 and 2021 are a part of us now. You don't need me to rehash the details of an overwhelming moment of global illness and social upheaval—you lived through it. Despite our moments of rage and desperation we managed to come together in new ways, learning to use video conferencing platforms, and masking up and socially distancing in order to gather safely. We generously shared resources, renewed our commitment to teaching for equity, and marched for justice around the world. After everything we have been through, I acknowledge that we deserve to heal, to take a break from pain and fear, to respectfully mourn the lives we have lost, while also taking moments for joy and celebration.

When you are ready, the beautiful work awaits you. The post-pandemic world is an invitation to create collective magic, to co-construct community with new sets of students who will look to you for hope and reassurance that the future can be better than the past. As you help students process historic and present injustices, they may wonder if a better world is possible. As educators, we dream a better world into existence every day, through our love, our words, and our lessons. Part of the magic consists of engaging students in creating a vision of the society in which they want to live, and teaching them the skills needed to become empowered change agents.

The great news is that anyone can be a change agent. Novice and veteran teachers alike can engage students in understanding their own identities, exploring their passions, and using their talents in order for their voices to be heard. Students can learn from historic and contemporary youth speaking out on social issues through art, poetry, music, social media, and youth journalism. Teachers have great power in helping students find and develop their own transformative voices. Teaching is the most rewarding profession in the world, and we have the great honor to work with energetic, optimistic, and compassionate young people. As evidence, I provide this powerful poem written by Rigo, an 8th grader in Los Angeles:

I too hear America singing
From the deserts to the mountains,
From the coastal waters to the plains,
From the suburban neighborhoods to the sprawling cities,
I too hear America singing

But I also hear America sobbing
From the cries of justice to the cries for equality,
From the cries of a weeping mother to the cries of a weeping infant
I hear America sobbing

There are also the screams of anger,
The screams of a child being separated from his family,
The screams of violence all over the country
And the screams of and for freedom

I too hear America

Young people are hungry for honest lessons that allow them to explore the multifaceted, sometimes horrific, other times amazing layers of humanity. So go out there and create some magic. Fill yourself with inspiration, tune out the noise, and remember that you and your students are powerful and unstoppable. A more just world awaits us.

Isabel Morales, Ed.D., Award-winning
Secondary Social Studies Educator Named
Teacher of the Year by the Los Angeles Unified School
District and the Los Angeles County Office of Education

About the Editors

Mary Amanda (Mandy) Stewart, Ph.D., is associate professor in the Department of Literacy and Learning at Texas Woman's University and focuses her research on critical literacy and language instruction for multilingual adolescents. She is also coauthor of *But Does This Work with English Learners? A Guide for English Language Arts Teachers, Grades 6–12*.

Christina Salazar, M.L.S., is a doctoral student in the Department of Literacy and Learning at Texas Woman's University. She is a school librarian at an elementary school near Dallas, Texas. Her passion is in authentic representation and critical pedagogy. Before becoming a librarian, Salazar taught high school science for several years. She has been accepted to present at AERA, ILA, and other regional conferences. She is currently serving on the Texas Bluebonnet Award Programming Committee and is an officer on the Texas Library Association's Latino Caucus.

Victor Antonio Lozada, M.M.E., is adjunct music education faculty at the University of North Texas–Dallas and has taught general music education for 13 years. He is a Ph.D. candidate in Reading at Texas Woman's University. Lozada's research focuses on the intersections among music, language, and critical literacies. You can read his work on music and critical literacies in *The Orff Echo* and *NABE Global Perspectives*. He also is an editorial board member of the music education online journal *Reverberations: Teachers Teaching Teachers*.

Christina Thomas, M.Ed., has been teaching pre-K for six years, and she was a teacher's assistant for two years prior to earning her teaching certification. She graduated with a B.A. in psychology and an M.A. in reading education.

Her certifications include generalist EC-6, reading specialist EC-12, and ESL supplemental EC-12. Thomas is a Ph.D. student in Reading at Texas Woman's University. She also works for her district's 21st-Century ACE Program as a teacher, and she is responsible for writing lesson plans for various ACE classes. Her research interests focus on early childhood literacy teaching and intervention and early writing development.

About the Contributors

Phyliciá Anderson, M.A., has taught high school English language arts, photojournalism, and creative writing for nine years. She has also worked with adolescents through sponsoring such extracurricular activities as the yearbook staff and the Black Student Union. She is also a Ph.D. student in reading education at Texas Woman's University. Anderson's research entails multiliteracy pedagogical practices for diverse learners. You can read her work on the intersection of multilingualism and multimodality in the *Texas English Language Teaching Journal*.

Juan Borda, M.Ed., is a doctoral student in the Department of Literacy and Learning at Texas Woman's University (TWU) in Denton, Texas, where he also received his M.Ed. and graduate certificate of biliteracy. He was an adjunct instructor in the bilingual/ESL program at TWU. He is a bilingual education teacher. Borda has taught emergent bilingual students for nineteen years in primarily transitional, developmental, and dual-language programs. His research interest is in biliteracy development through integrating multi-modalities with a sociocultural approach.

Yismelle Duran, M.Sc., is a multilingual world languages teacher at the high school level. She has studied law, international affairs, and globalization and development. Originally from the Dominican Republic, she has also lived in the United States and Belgium. Duran is a Ph.D. candidate in reading at Texas Woman's University. Her research focus is multilingualism, heritage language maintenance, and multiliteracies.

Patricia Flint, Ph.D., is a graduate research assistant in the College of Professional Education and a special education doctoral candidate at Texas

Woman's University. She has been in the educational field since 2003 and since then has been a teacher, assistant principal, and special education supervisor. Flint has published in academic journals and contributed to other books, including a chapter in TESOL's Transforming Practices for the High School Classroom, *Picture This! Using Illustrated Books to Support Comprehension of Social Studies Complex Texts.*

Mariannella Núñez, Ph.D., is assistant professor of teacher education at the University of the Incarnate Word. Her research interests are guided by sociocritical perspectives and driven by the desire to amplify the stories of marginalized and minoritized communities. She has taught in elementary bilingual and ESL settings for ten years and also taught adolescent newcomers in high schools.

Margarita Ramos-Rivera, M.Ed., has taught bilingual/ESL and dual language for twenty-two years. She has worked with different age groups fostering love for reading and is part of the Curriculum Translator Team of Denton ISD. She is also a Ph.D. student in reading at Texas Woman's University. Ramos-Rivera's research interests include bilingual/dual language/ESL education, critical literacy, and adolescent literacy.

Marlene Walker, M.A., has taught bilingual/ESL and dual language for seventeen years. She has worked with different age groups throughout her career, sponsoring folkloric dance as an extracurricular activity. She is also a Ph.D. student in the Department of Literacy and Learning at Texas Woman's University. Walker's research interests include bilingual/dual language/ESL education, critical literacy, social justice, and Spanish language instruction.

www.ingramcontent.com/pod-product-compliance
Lightning Source LLC
Chambersburg PA
CBHW022012300426
44117CB00005B/147